Principles of Rule-Based Programming

Thom Frühwirth

AF288527

Thom Frühwirth is a professor of Computer Science at Ulm University, Germany. His research areas are rule-based programming and constraint reasoning. He is the designer of the logical formalism and programming language Constraint Handling Rules.

The cover illustration shows a coloring of a mason's mark by our rule-based AI drawing generation tool VanDeGraphGenerator [35].

Bibliografische Information der Deutschen Nationalbibliothek: Die Deutsche Nationalbibliothek verzeichnet diese Publikation in der Deutschen Nationalbibliografie; detaillierte bibliografische Daten sind im Internet über dnb.dnb.de abrufbar.

Die automatisierte Analyse des Werkes, um daraus Informationen insbesondere über Muster, Trends und Korrelationen gemäß §44b UrhG („Text und Data Mining") zu gewinnen, ist untersagt.

Verlag: BoD · Books on Demand GmbH, In de Tarpen 42, 22848 Norderstedt, bod@bod.de
Druck: Libri Plureos GmbH, Friedensallee 273, 22763 Hamburg

ISBN 978-3-7693-7633-3

Principles of Rule-Based Programming

Thom Frühwirth

The book provides a unified overview of concepts and features of a comprehensive variety of rule-based programming languages. They have applications in diverse areas such as workflow systems, the Semantic Web, decision support, optimization problems, simulation and modeling, software engineering, program verification and security, and artificial intelligence.

Through clear definitions, helpful explanations, concrete examples and instructive exercises with selected solutions, the reader will gain a thorough understanding of rule-based formalisms, systems and programming languages.

The rule-based formalisms presented are Multiset Transformation, Term Rewriting Systems, Colored Petri Nets and Logical Algorithms. The rule-based systems are Production Rules, Event-Condition-Action Rules and Datalog. The rule-based programming languages are Functional Programming, Constraint Logic Programming and Concurrent Constraint Programming.

By embedding these approaches into Constraint Handling Rules, a powerful and versatile programming language, it provides a common platform for understanding and comparison as well as execution and analysis of rule-based approaches.

The book is ideal for researchers, students and programmers who want to learn about the power and potential of rule-based programming and understand its characteristic features and abilities.

For a quick start on programming in Constraint Handling Rules, check out the online demo at `http://chrjs.net/`

Contents

III   RULE-BASED SYSTEMS   81

12 Production Rules (PR)   85

13 Event-Condition-Action (ECA) Rules   107

14 Logical Algorithms (LA)   117

15 Datalog (DL)   127

Chapter 1

Introduction: Rule-Based Approaches

Rule-based approaches are a powerful tool for manipulating data in a variety of contexts. Rules consist of a pattern which is a description of some data, as well as a statement specifying how that data should be replaced or transformed if it matches the pattern. Rule applications are repeated until no further changes are made to the data.

Rule-based approaches vary from theoretical formalisms such as term rewriting systems, to practical declarative programming languages such as Haskell and Prolog, to pragmatic rule-based systems such as CLIPS, JESS and Drools.

This book introduces rule-based formalisms, systems, and programming languages by embedding them in Constraint Handling Rules (CHR).

1.1 Applications of Rule-Based Approaches

Rule-based approaches have applications in diverse areas such as workflow systems, the Semantic Web, data transformation, expert systems and decision support, optimization problems, simulation and modeling, program analysis, software engineering, verification and security, and artificial intelligence.

For example, rule-based approaches have seen significant adoption as business rules for workflow systems. These systems encode and enforce the rules and policies of an organization to manage the flow of work and the allocation of resources.

Rule-based approaches are also applied in software engineering, for example in UML (Unified Modeling Language), the standard language for modeling software systems, to enforce invariants and other constraints on UML models. Another application area is in model transformation to analyse, transform and refine software models towards an implementation.

Another area where rule-based approaches have seen widespread use is in the Semantic Web. The Semantic Web is a vision of the World Wide Web in which data is annotated with machine-readable semantics, enabling more effective interoperability and reasoning between systems.

In machine learning, rule-based approaches can complement neural nets like LLM's (Large Language Models) to tame hallucinations, enforce consistency, and enable reasoning and explanation.

1.2 Embedding Rule-Based Approaches in CHR

In this book, we present concrete embeddings of a comprehensive variety of rule-based approaches in CHR. CHR is a powerful and versatile programming language that combines the declarativity of logic and constraint reasoning with the practicality of rule-based systems.

Embedding of programming languages means representing the syntax and semantics of one programming language within another programming language. Our embeddings are based on straightforward source-to-source translation of programs in rule-based approaches to equivalent CHR programs. Source-to-source translation refers to the translation between program texts without intermediate representation.

Our embeddings allow for the use of the features and constructs of the embedded language within CHR. It enables to add new functionality to languages and to facilitate interoperability between different languages. In this way, CHR provides a common platform for execution and analysis. It enables cross-fertilization of the approaches by the direct comparison based on their CHR implementations, and opens up possibilities for combining them in novel ways.

In this book, we first introduce Constraint Handling Rules (CHR) as the common basis for rule-based programming. Then we discuss the following three kinds of rule-based approaches and their embeddings in CHR.

- *Rule-based formalisms* include GAMMA Multiset Transformation, Term Rewriting Systems (TRS), and Colored Petri Nets (CPN). These formalisms explicitly or implicitly use *rewrite rules* to transform terms or graph structures. We also introduce Functional Programming (FP) languages like Haskell under the heading of formalisms because FP can be derived from TRS.

- *Rule-based systems* include Production Rules (PR) like OPS5 and Drools, and Event-Condition-Action (ECA) Rules as well as Logical Algorithms (LA) and Datalog (DL). These systems use if-then rules to describe how to transform data represented as facts.

- *Rule-based programming languages* besides FP include Constraint Logic Programming (CLP) languages like Prolog and Concurrent Constraint Programming (CCP). These programming languages use logical inference rules for inference and constraint solving.

Some embeddings of rule-based approaches into CHR have been discussed in research publications and have been refined for more than a decade of lecturing. In this book, the transformations are defined and explained in detail, they are made concrete, correct, complete and comparable.

Chapter 2

Prelude: Ancient Rules

The explicit employment of logic and rules goes back more than 2000 years, to ancient Greece, where the philosopher Aristotle thought about how to reason correctly and express this process by rules. Over the centuries, the approach was refined. The invention of machines for arithmetic calculation also paved the way for the mechanization of logical reasoning, resulting in the computer as universal computation device.

Aristotle (384-322 B.C.) investigated the nature of argumentation as logical inference. In a dialogue, what can be directly inferred from accepted facts? Which consequences cannot be disputed, because they follow merely syntactical, independent of the semantics of the facts considered? Aristotle devised patterns of inference called syllogisms, which are rules about elementary relationships between entities. In his work *Prior Analytics*, Aristotle defines:

> „A syllogism is discourse in which, certain things being having been supposed, something different from the things supposed results of necessity from their being so. I mean by the last phrase that they produce the consequence, and by this, that no further term is required from without in order to make the consequence necessary."

More concretely, a *syllogism* (Greek: conclusion, inference) is an inference rule that draws a conclusion based on two premises. Each of its three components is a sentence with a subject and a predicate. Each pair of components shares exactly one of those entities (subjects or predicates). So there are three different entities in a syllogism. For example:

Major premise:	All men are mortal.
Minor premise:	Socrates is a man.
Conclusion:	Socrates is mortal.

Logic was dominated by syllogistic reasoning until the 19th century, though it was very limited in its application. In 1865, Austrian playwright Franz Grillparzer wrote the epigram:

> Der Syllogismus wäre ein rechter Schatz,
> Hätte man nur immer einen ersten Satz,
> Doch nimmt man einen falschen oder ungewissen,
> Wächst der Irrtum im richtigen Schließen.

> The syllogism would be a real treasure,
> If only one always had a right premise,
> But if one takes a false or uncertain one,
> The error grows despite the correct inference.

In the 20th century, significant advances in theory and practice of logical reasoning were made. Researchers investigated its formal nature and the notion of computability as early as 1930. The 1940s saw the development of the first computers, driven by military applications during the Second World War. With the theoretical work came the formalisms and with computers came the programming languages. We only mention some early rule-based approaches here. Already in the late 1950s, Lisp was introduced, considered by many as the first functional programming language. In the early 1960s, the formalism of Petri Nets was conceived. The early 1970s saw the advent of formal term rewriting, practical production rule systems and logic programming languages. Some remarks on the history of rule-based programming will be made in the upcoming chapters for each approach, in detail in Chapter 12 on Production Rules.

Part I

CONSTRAINT HANDLING RULES (CHR)

Constraint Handling Rules (CHR) are a declarative programming language and a logical reasoning formalism. CHR bridges the gap between logical specification and executable program by rewriting constraints. A *constraint* is a logical predicate that represents some piece of information or a condition that must be satisfied. By the notion of constraint, CHR does not distinguish between data and operations, rules are both descriptive and executable. CHR has the ability of abstract execution with incomplete information expressed by constraints on logical variables. This helps confluence checking as well as partial evaluation and program transformation.

CHR programs have a number of desirable properties guaranteed (such as implementing anytime online algorithms) and can be analyzed for other important properties (such as confluence and program equivalence). CHR allows algorithms to be implemented with best known time and space complexity, something that is not known to be possible in other pure declarative programming languages. Optimizing CHR compilers have demonstrated its efficiency by competing well with other rule-based systems and programming languages.

CHR has been used for applications in constraint solving and reasoning, type systems, cognitive systems, bio-informatics, abductive reasoning, multi-agent systems, decision support, natural language processing and computational linguistics, compilation, scheduling and time tabling, spatio-temporal reasoning, verification and testing, semantic web, and data mining.

Commercial applications include financial services (SecuritEase, New Zealand), injection mould design (Cornerstone Intelligent Software Corp, Canada), optical network design (Mitre, USA), enterprise applications (LogicBlox, USA), unit testing for Java (Agitar Software, USA), health management (new ocean, USA), and software verification (GSSE, Germany). See Section 7 in [69] for details.

Chapter 3

Syntax and Semantics

As with any language, rule-based approaches can be formally defined by their syntax and semantics. The *syntax* states how the constituents of a language ought to be combined to form valid statements and the *semantics* gives meaning to these statements. The abstract description of what it means to execute certain programming language statements is called an *operational semantics*, while the *declarative semantics* describes the meaning as a formula in some logic. We assume familiarity with first-order predicate logic throughout this book.

We will define the abstract syntax, the declarative semantics and the abstract operational semantics of CHR based on [38, 31]. We also discuss the more implementation-oriented refined operational semantics typically realized in practical sequential implementations of CHR [23]. For parallel and concurrent CHR see [34].

3.1 Abstract Syntax

The CHR language is based on the abstract concept of constraints. *Constraints* are relations, predicates of first-order predicate logic. We distinguish two kinds of constraints: *built-in (predefined) constraints* from the underlying host language and *user-defined (CHR) constraints* which are defined by the rules in a CHR program. There are at least the built-in constraints *true* and *false*, syntactic equality $=$ over terms including lists and multisets, and the usual relations over arithmetic

11

expressions. Let $\mathcal{CT}$ be a logical theory for the built-in constraints. The arguments of constraints are terms. We will need the standard notions of substitutions, matching and instances for terms.

Def. 3.1.1 (Terms and Substitutions) A *term* is defined inductively as follows: A variable is a term. If f is a function symbol of arity $n \geq 0$ and $t_1, \ldots, t_n$ are terms, then $f(t_1, \ldots, t_n)$ is a term. The t_i are called *arguments* of the term. A *subterm* of a term is an argument or a subterm of an argument of the term. If f has arity 0, we call it a constant and write just f instead of $f()$. A term is *ground* if it does not contain any variables.

A *substitution* θ is a finite unary function written in postfix notation that replaces variables by terms. When a substitution is applied to a term, it is applied at once to all variables in the term. Given a substitution θ such that $X\theta \neq X$, we say that $X\theta$ is *bound* or has a *binding*. A term s is an *instance* of a term t if $s = t\theta$, we say that s *matches* t. ∎

We use upper-case letters from the beginning of the alphabet to denote (possibly empty) conjunctions of constraints.

Def. 3.1.2 (CHR Syntax) A *CHR program* is a finite set of *generalized simpagation rules* of the form

$$r : H_1 \setminus H_2 \Leftrightarrow C \mid B$$

where r is an optional *name* (a unique identifier) of a rule. In the rule the *head* (left-hand side), H_1 and H_2 are conjunctions of CHR constraints, the optional *guard* C is a conjunction of built-in constraints, and the *body* (right-hand side) B is a goal. A *goal* is a conjunction of built-in and CHR constraints. The *local variables of a rule* are those not occurring in the rule head.

In a simpagation rule, H_1 are called the *kept constraints*, while H_2 are called the *removable constraints*. At least one of H_1 and H_2 must be non-empty conjunctions. If H_1 is empty, the rule corresponds to a *simplification rule*, also written

$$s : H_2 \Leftrightarrow C \mid B.$$

If H_2 is empty, the rule corresponds to a *propagation rule*, also written

$$p : H_1 \Rightarrow C \,|\, B.$$

We may write a generalized simpagation rule as *generalized simplification rule*

$$r : H_1 \wedge H_2 \Leftrightarrow C \,|\, H_1 \wedge B.$$

∎

Conjunctions are understood as multisets of their single constraints. Empty conjunctions are equivalent to the built-in constraint *true*. To avoid clutter, we often use simple commas to denote logical conjunction.

3.2 Declarative Semantics

A declarative semantics associates a program with a logical theory. This logical reading should coincide with the intended meaning of program. In this way, the declarative semantics facilitates nontrivial program analysis (e.g., correctness with regard to a logical specification, and for program transformation).

The declarative semantics of CHR is based on first-order predicate logic, where constraints are viewed as predicates and rules as logical equivalences. The logical reading of a CHR program consists of the logical reading of its rules and built-ins.

Def. 3.2.1 (CHR Declarative Semantics) A generalized simpagation rule corresponds to a logical equivalence

$$\mathcal{CT} \models \forall (H_1 \wedge H_2 \wedge \exists C \leftrightarrow H_1 \wedge C \wedge \exists B).$$

where all variables are universally quantified except those occurring only in the guard C or only in the body B. These variables are existentially quantified. ∎

The operational and declarative semantics should coincide. Soundness means the result of computation according to the operational semantics is correct regarding to declarative semantics. Completeness means every logical consequence according to the declarative semantics can also be computed. Theorems show that for CHR, the semantics are strongly related, because all states in a derivation are logically equivalent. Completeness cannot be fully achieved, because first-order logic is too powerful.

3.3 Abstract Operational Semantics

Computations in CHR and in rule-based approaches in general are sequences of rule applications. Structural operational semantics are defined using a *transition system* between states that contain statements of the programming language. For CHR, states are conjunctions of constraints and transitions correspond to rule applications.

Def. 3.3.1 (Abstract Operational Semantics) A *state* S is a pair $\langle G, C \rangle$, where G is a goal (store) and C is a constraint (store) for built-in constraints. An *initial state (query)* is a state of the form $\langle G, true \rangle$. A state is called *successful final state (answer)* if it is of the form $\langle E, C \rangle$ and no transition is possible, and if C is different from *false*. A state is called *failed final state (answer)* if it is of the form $\langle G, false \rangle$.

A *copy (renaming, variant)* of a state, term or rule is obtained by uniformly substituting its variables by new variables. We then say that the variables have been *renamed apart*.

We define the following two transitions:

Apply

If $\quad (A \backslash B \Leftrightarrow D \mid H)$ is a copy of a rule in P with variables $\bar{x}$

and $\quad \mathcal{CT} \models \forall\, (C \rightarrow \exists \bar{x}((A \backslash B) = (E \backslash F) \wedge D))$

then $\quad \langle E \wedge F \wedge G, C \rangle \mapsto \langle E \wedge H \wedge G, ((A \backslash B) = (E \backslash F)) \wedge D \wedge C \rangle$

Solve

If $\quad \mathcal{CT} \models (C \wedge D_1) \leftrightarrow D_2$

then $\quad \langle C \wedge G, D_1 \rangle \mapsto \langle G, D_2 \rangle$

A *computation (derivation)* of a query S is a connected sequence $S_i \mapsto_{r_i} S_{i+1}$ beginning with the query S as *initial state* S_0 and either ending in a *final state (answer, result)* S_n or *not terminating (diverging)*. If the final state is failed we say the computation *failed*.

The remainder of the goal, G, is called *context* of the rule application. It remains unchanged. It may be empty.

The relation $\mapsto^*$ denotes the reflexive and transitive closure of the transition relation $\mapsto$. ∎

The **Solve** transition moves a built-in constraint from the goal store to the constraint store which will be simplified in the process.

The **Apply** transition needs more explanation. It applies a renamed-apart copy of a generalized simpagation rule from the given program. The rule is applicable if its head constraints are matched by constraints in the state one-by-one and if, under this matching, the guard check of the rule holds. This is logically expressed by the *precondition* $\mathcal{CT} \models \forall\, (C \to \exists \bar{x}((A \backslash B)=(E \backslash F) \wedge D))$.

We now explain the meaning of the precondition in more detail. A CHR constraint *matches* another CHR constraint H if it is an instance of H, i.e. H serves as a pattern. In that case, the constraints can be syntactically equated so that only variables in the H are bound by the equality. So the equation $\exists \bar{x}((A \backslash B)=(E \backslash F))$ means pairwise matching of the CHR constraints of $(E \backslash F)$ to $(A \backslash B)$. In the precondition, the *guard check* holds if the guard D of the rule together with the equation for matching is logically implied by the built-in constraints C in the state. If the guard is ground, the guard check amounts to a simple test.

The rule application replaces the matched removable CHR constraints F in the goal store by the body of the rule and adds the equation $(A \backslash B)=(E \backslash F)$ and the guard to the constraint store. Rules are applied until exhaustion, until no more rule application is possible. This holds for all rule-based approaches that we discuss. Note that the abstract semantics does not account for termination of propagation rules. If a state can fire a propagation rule once, it can do so again and again.

3.4 Refined Operational Semantics

The abstract operational semantics has been further detailed in the *refined operational semantics* of CHR [23] which is a concretization of the abstract operational semantics for implementations. This means that every computation in the refined semantics has a corresponding computation in the abstract semantics, but the converse does not always hold. The refined semantics of CHR deals with termination of propagation rules and also fixes the order of rule applications and of constraint evaluation in a goal.

Constraints in a goal are evaluated in reading order going from left to right. So the left-most constraint will be executed first. A CHR constraint under execution is called *active*. It behaves like a procedure that goes through the rules of the program in the order they are written in order to find applicable rules. When it matches a head constraint of a rule, it will look for constraints in the goal store that match the remaining head constraints and check the guard until the first applicable rule is found. To improve termination behavior and efficiency, the removable head constraints of the generalized simpagation rule are matched first.

When a rule is applied, the constraints that matched its removable constraints are removed and the rule body is executed. When a propagation rule is applied, the matched constraints are recorded in a propagation history to ensure that it is not applied a second time in the same way.

Afterwards, if the active constraint has not been removed in the rule application, the next rule in the program will be tried with it. After trying all rules, the active constraint, if still present, will become inactive and visible for future active constraints. It will become active again when its variables are further constrained or bound, because then guards of rules may now hold and make them applicable.

Here is a simple example of a CHR program. In examples, we will use the concrete syntax of CHR hosted in the logic programming language Prolog. For variable names we use upper-case letters from the end of the alphabet.

Example 3.4.1 (Minimum) The rule below computes the minimum of a multiset of numbers n_i, given as the query $\mathtt{min}(n_1)$, $\mathtt{min}(n_2)$,..., $\mathtt{min}(n_k)$. Each CHR constraint $\mathtt{min}(n_i)$ means that the number n_i is a candidate for the minimum value.

```
min(N) \ min(M) <=> N=<M | true.
```

The simpagation rule takes two `min` candidates and removes the one with the larger value. It keeps going until only one, the smallest value, remains as single `min` constraint denoting the minimum. The program illustrates the use of rules with several head constraints instead of explicit loops or recursion for iteration over data. This keeps the program text compact and makes it easier to analyze it. The rule corresponds to the intuitive algorithm that when we are to find the minimum from a given list of numbers, we just cross out larger numbers until one, the minimum, remains.

Consider the query `min(1),min(0),min(2),min(1)`. A computation under the refined CHR semantics proceeds as follows: We execute the first constraint of the query `min(1)`, it becomes active. The remaining constraints of the query are not processed yet. So the rule for minimum cannot apply, because it needs two constraints that match its head. So `min(1)` becomes inactive and is kept in the store. Let us look in more detail how the computation continues:

- The second constraint from the query, `min(0)`, becomes active.
- It tries the rule `min(N) \ min(M) <=> N=<M | true`.
- It first matches the removable head constraint `min(M)` with M=0.
- Next we look for a match for the other head constraint.
- Indeed, the inactive `min(1)` matches `min(N)` with N=1.
- We check the guard of the rule N=<M, i.e. 1=<0. It does not hold.
- Therefore the matchings are undone.
- Next `min(0)` matches the kept head of the rule `min(N)` with N=0.
- And `min(1)` matches the other head `min(M)` with M=1.
- The guard N=<M, i.e. 0=<1, does hold now.
- The rule is applied, `min(1)` is removed and `true` is executed.
- For `min(0)`, there are no more head constraints to match and no more rules to try, it becomes inactive and is kept in the store.
- The next constraint from the query `min(2)` becomes active,...

It is less cumbersome to conveniently summarize the computation:

$$\underline{\texttt{min(1)}}, \underline{\texttt{min(0)}}, \texttt{min(2)}, \texttt{min(1)} \mapsto$$
$$\underline{\texttt{min(0)}}, \underline{\texttt{min(2)}}, \texttt{min(1)} \mapsto$$
$$\underline{\texttt{min(0)}}, \underline{\texttt{min(1)}} \mapsto$$
$$\texttt{min(0)}$$

For clarity we underlined the constraints that are involved in a rule application. The currently active constraint has a double underline. The final state means that the minimum of the numbers $1, 0, 2, 1$ is 0.

3.5 Implementations

CHR is often integrated into existing programming languages as a language extension that blends in with the syntax of its host language, be it Prolog, Lisp, Haskell, C [79], C++ [11], Java or Javascript [57]. In the host language, CHR constraints can be posted and inspected, and in the CHR rules, host language statements can be included.

The first wide-spread implementations of CHR were in Prolog and based on [49]. Many CHR implementations today - be it in Prolog, Java or C - are based on [79, 74]. Such state-of-the-art CHR libraries allow to implement any algorithm with time and space consumption that is typically within an order of magnitude from the best-known implementations in imperative programming language [67, 73].

Actually, [67] has proven that every algorithm can be implemented in CHR with the best known time and space complexity. CHR with mode declarations achieves the optimal time and space complexity as do imperative languages. On the other hand, the declarative programming languages pure Prolog and strict Haskell have a time complexity which is a polylogarithmic factor from optimal, and their space complexity is not optimal.

CLIPS (in C) and JESS (in Java) are considered by many to be the most efficient rule-based systems. The benchmarks of [73] show that a Java implementation of CHR as well as CHR in C (CCHR) [79] are faster than CLIPS and JESS, sometimes by several orders of magnitude. The CHR implementations allow to apply millions of rules per second.

One reason for the effectiveness of CHR is that it uses a compiler and runtime system that is a significant advancement over existing algorithms for rule applications (such as RETE, TREAT, LEAPS) for executing rule-based languages [73]. Besides indexing on constraint arguments, CHR compilers use sophisticated optimizations such as memory reuse, late storage, guard optimization and join ordering optimization [50, 73, 42].

Chapter 4

Properties of Programs and Their Analysis

CHR programs have a number of desirable properties guaranteed and can be analyzed for others. Any CHR program will by nature be monotonic in rule applications and implement an anytime approximation and online (incremental) algorithm. After introducing these properties, we then shortly discuss the analysis of termination and time complexity and in more detail confluence with completion and operational program equivalence of CHR programs. These properties and analysis results hold for the abstract CHR semantics, they can be weakened by the refined semantics of implementations.

4.1 Monotonicity Properties

In the abstract operational semantics we can observe two types of monotonicity for rule applications that help incremental program development, program execution and program analysis.

First, adding rules to a program cannot inhibit the applicability of any rules. Already a program with a few first rules is executable, and we can add rules to cover more and more cases, enabling more and more desired computations. This aids incremental program development and rapid prototyping. Moreover, the confluence test discussed below can discover situations where old and new rules lead to different results. Completion offers a way to resolve such conflicts by introducing additional rules.

Second, adding constraints to a state cannot inhibit rule applications. During a rule application, the context of the state stays unchanged. We can actually change it without influencing the rule application itself. So if a rule is applicable in a state, it is also applicable in any larger state where constraints have been added as long as the state is consistent [6]. Clearly such context-independence does not hold in imperative programming languages, where the context may update shared data, resulting in write conflicts.

4.2 Anytime and Online Algorithm Properties

The *anytime algorithm property* means that we can interrupt the execution of a program at any time and observe the current state as an approximation to the intermediate result. We can then continue directly from this state, without the need to recompute from scratch. If we interrupt again, we will observe another intermediate state that is closer to the final result than the one before. The intermediate results more and more approximate the final answer. By this description, an anytime algorithm is also an *approximation algorithm*. This properties directly follow from the operational semantics as a state transition system.

The *online (incremental) algorithm property* means that we can add additional constraints while the program is running without the need to recompute from scratch. The program will behave as if the newly added constraints were present from the beginning but have been ignored so far. This property is an immediate consequence of the monotonicity property of CHR.

4.3 Termination and Time Complexity Analysis

Termination in CHR is undecidable due to the Turing-completeness of the programming language. One way to show termination is to prove that in each rule, if the guard holds, the rule head is strictly larger than the rule body using some well-founded termination order.

For CHR programs that mainly use simplification rules, simple orders are often sufficient to prove termination [27, 28]. More sophisticated methods are needed in the presence of propagation rules [59, 60, 33]. Also an approximation of CHR programs by constraint logic programs (CLP) has been used to analyse the termination behavior of CHR [48].

The runtime of a CHR program not only depends on the number of rule applications (derivation length), but also on the number of rule application attempts. The meta-complexity theorem in [29] basically states that the *time complexity* is bounded by the derivation length taken to the power of the maximum number of heads in a rule. This only gives crude upper bounds. For CHR, there is a more realistic meta-complexity theorem derived from that of the Logical Algorithms (LA) formalism [20].

4.4 Confluence Analysis and Completion

Confluence of a program guarantees that the answer to a query is always the same, no matter which of the applicable rules are applied during computation. This means that while the computation may be nondeterministic in the rule choice, the result of the computation is deterministic, it is a function of the initial state. There is a decidable, sufficient and necessary syntactic condition for confluence of terminating CHR programs [6]. That paper shows that confluent programs always implement anytime online algorithms and can be executed in parallel without modification. Furthermore, confluence implies a consistent declarative program semantics and improves the soundness and completeness results between the operational and declarative semantics.

The idea of the confluence test is to construct a finite number of so-called critical states from the heads and guards of rules in the program such that after applying one rule, the other rule is no longer applicable. One then checks if these conflicting rule applications can be continued with computations that lead to equivalent states. If this is the case for all critical states in the program, we have proven confluence. Otherwise we have found a counter-example to confluence.

Def. 4.4.1 (Critical State and Critical Pair) Given two (not necessarily different) generalized simpagation rules whose variables have been renamed apart. Let A_1 and A_2 be non-empty conjunctions of CHR constraints taken from the two heads, respectively.

A *critical state* of the two rules is the conjunction of the heads and guards of the two rules where A_1 has been replaced by the syntactic equality $A_1=A_2$.

The *critical pair* are the two states that come from applying the two rules to the critical state. ■

The critical states are constructed so that there is a conflict if at least one rule removes constraints from A_1 or A_2, because then the other rule is no longer applicable.

A terminating CHR program is *confluent* if and only if all its critical pairs are joinable [1, 6]. A critical pair is *joinable* if there are computations for its two states that lead to states that are equivalent. Thus a critical pair is trivially joinable if its built-in constraints are inconsistent or if it is between two propagation rules. Decidability of confluence for terminating CHR programs comes from the fact that there is only a finite number of critical pairs to consider.

Example 4.4.1 (Coin Flip, Confluence) Consider a coin-toss simulator defined by the two rules

```
flip(Coin) <=> true | Coin = head.
flip(Coin) <=> true | Coin = tail.
```

The program handles the constraint `flip(Coin)` by committing to one of the rules, thereby equating either `head` or `tail` with the variable `Coin`. The critical state

$$flip(Coin), flip(Coin)=flip(Coin), true, true$$

yields the following critical pair:

$$Coin=head <> Coin=tail$$

These two states are final and different, hence not *joinable*. So the program is not confluent.

4.4.1 Completion Method

Completion is the process of adding rules to a non-confluent program until it becomes confluent [3]. Completion can be also used for program specialization [5]. The rules are generated between the states of non-joinable critical pairs in order to join them. The generation of such rules is not always possible. It may also introduce new critical pairs. Thus the completion process may not be terminating.

4.5 Operational Program Equivalence Analysis

A fundamental and hard question in programming language semantics is when two programs should be considered equivalent. For example correctness of program transformations can be studied only with respect to a notion of equivalence. Program equivalence can also be used to discover redundant code in a program.

Operational (program) equivalence means that given two programs, any query leads to equivalent states in both programs. There is a decidable, sufficient and necessary syntactic condition for operational equivalence of terminating and confluent CHR programs [4]. As far as we know, CHR is the only programming language in practical use with a decidable test for operational equivalence.

The test for operational equivalence of terminating and confluent CHR programs is straightforward. The heads and guards of all rules in both programs are each evaluated as queries in both programs, and for each such query, the computations must reach equivalent states in both programs.

Chapter 5

Program Transformation

Program transformation refers to the process of modifying a program in some systematic way to produce another equivalent or semantically related program. Program transformation can be used for optimizing program performance, improving code readability, adapting a program to run on different hardware or software, or for introducing new features. Program transformation is abundant in CHR [40, 2, 69, 32]. Methods exist for unfolding rules [44], for specializing rules with regard to a specific given query [30], and for optimizations induced by completion [5, 3]. Recently, runtime repeated recursion unfolding was introduced with CHR as a systematic strategy to achieve super-linear speedups [37].

Source-to-source translation refers to the translation between program texts without intermediate representation. Many CHR extensions have been implemented in this way in CHR itself. These include nonmonotonic negation-as-absence [75], aggregates [68] and rules with probabilities [39, 19, 66].

Partial evaluation is a specific program transformation technique which produces a new program by evaluating some statements in the original program and replacing them with the results. This can optimize the resulting program by reducing the computations it needs to perform. It can also specialize the program for a particular set of inputs. In CHR, *rule simplification* is an auxiliary technique that simplifies the representation of a rule, independent of the program in which it appears.

5.1 Rule Simplification

Rule simplification is a CHR program transformation that replaces a rule with a simpler more efficient yet semantically equivalent form. It simplifies the built-in constraints of a rule, maximizes the number of kept constraints and removes superfluous rules [37]. We assume all types of CHR rules have been rewritten into generalized simplification rules.

Def. 5.1.1 (CHR Rule Simplification) Given a generalized simplification rule r of the form

$$r : H \Leftrightarrow C \mid D \wedge B,$$

where D are the built-in constraints and B are the CHR constraints in the rule body.

Rule simplification replaces rule r by the following generalized simpagation rule

$$(r' : H_1' \setminus H_2' \Leftrightarrow C' \mid D' \wedge B_2')$$

where C' and D' are built-in constraints and where H_1', H_2' and B_2' are CHR constraints.

In CHR head constraints, terms can be replaced by terms that are syntactically equivalent according to C. In CHR body constraints, terms can be replaced by terms that are syntactically equivalent according to $C \wedge D$. These replacement should maximize the common CHR constraints H_1' of head and body. Then H_2' is the result of removing H_1' from the head and B_2' is the result of removing H_1' from the body.

The built-in constraints C' are the result of simplifying the guard C. D' is the result of simplifying $C \wedge D$, the body built-in constraints with the guard temporarily added, and then removing the built-in constraints that are logically implied by the guard C.

Next, remove the resulting generalized simpagation rule r' as redundant if it is of one of the two forms

$$K \setminus H \Leftrightarrow false \mid B \text{ or } K \setminus \Leftrightarrow C \mid true.$$

Finally, the remaining rule is written as a simplification or propagation rule if possible. ∎

In the given rule, we replace head and guard as well as the body by simpler yet semantically equivalent goals. Built-in constraints are simplified. Terms in constraints can be replaced by ones that are equivalent according to the built-in constraints. We temporarily add the guard C when we simplify the body for correctness and to improve the simplification. For example, $X \leq Y \mid X \geq Y$ becomes $X \leq Y \mid X = Y$. From the result, we remove built-in constraints that are implied by the guard. For example, $X \leq Y, Z = 0 \mid X = Y, Z \geq 0$ becomes $X \leq Y, Z = 0 \mid X = Y$.

If a CHR constraint from the given head and a CHR constraint from the body are syntactically equivalent when the built-in constraints of the guard and body hold, then we remove both constraints and place one of them in the kept head. Finally, we remove rules that are superfluous. The rules with inconsistent guard can never apply, and a propagation rule with body $true$ does not change the state when applied.

For an example of rule simplification, consider the rule

$$c(X, Y) \setminus c(X, X) \Leftrightarrow X \leq Y \mid X \geq Y \wedge c(Y, Y).$$

It is turned into a generalized simplification rule

$$c(X, Y) \wedge c(X, X) \Leftrightarrow X \leq Y \mid X \geq Y \wedge c(X, Y) \wedge c(Y, Y).$$

The guard $X \leq Y$ and the body built-in $X \geq Y$ together imply $X = Y$. Therefore the body built-in is simplified into $X = Y$. Now that $X = Y$, the body constraints $c(X, Y) \wedge c(Y, Y)$ become equivalent to the head constraints $c(X, Y) \wedge c(X, X)$. Thus we can rewrite the rule into a propagation rule

$$c(X, Y) \wedge c(X, X) \Rightarrow X \leq Y \mid X = Y.$$

5.2 Partial Evaluation

Partial evaluation for CHR replaces the body of a rule by the result of evaluating its kept head constraints, guard and body in the given program and applying rule simplification.

Def. 5.2.1 (CHR Partial Evaluation) Given a terminating and confluent CHR program with a rule written in the form of a generalized simplification rule

$$r : H \iff C \,|\, D,$$

then a *partial evaluation* of rule r is the rule simplification of the rule

$$r' : H \iff C \,|\, E,$$

where $C \wedge D \mapsto^* E$. The variables of the head are taken as non-local variables in the evaluation. ∎

Since the program is terminating and confluent, it can be shown that the given rule and its partial evaluation are operationally equivalent. Hence we can replace the former with the latter in the program. Note that E need not be a final state.

Chapter 6

Introductory Examples

We present different programming styles and evaluation methods in CHR: multiset transformation, top-down and bottom-up evaluation. The following CHR examples are explained and analyzed in detail in Chapter 7 of the book [31].

6.1 Multiset Transformation

Algorithms based on *multiset transformation* rewrite multisets of data. In CHR, data is represented by CHR constraints. The minimum program we already introduced is an example of multiset transformation.

Example 6.1.1 (Greatest Common Divisor) We implement a variation of the Euclidean algorithm to compute the greatest common divisor (GCD) of positive natural (and rational) numbers that are each written as gcd(N).

```
gcd(N) \ gcd(M) <=> 0<N,N<M | gcd(M-N).
```

After exhaustive rule application, the remaining gcd constraints will be identical and contain the answer. Consider a query gcd(15), gcd(6) and its computation:

gcd(15), gcd(6) ↦
gcd(6), gcd(9) ↦

$$\frac{\underline{\text{gcd}(6)},\ \underline{\underline{\text{gcd}(3)}} \mapsto}{\text{gcd}(3),\ \text{gcd}(3)}$$

So the GCD of 15 and 6 is 3. The GCD program also works for more than two numbers due to monotonicity and incrementality of CHR and confluence of the program.

Example 6.1.2 (Prime Numbers Sieve of Eratosthenes)   We implement the algorithm known as the Sieve of Eratosthenes, but without any particular sifting order. A rule that just removes multiples of numbers suffices.

```
prime(I) \ prime(J) <=> 0 is J mod I | true.
```

The built-in constraint `V is E` in infix notation evaluates the arithmetic expression `E` and syntactically equates the result with variable `V`.

To compute prime numbers, the query contains all numbers from 2 up to N in the form `prime(2), prime(3), prime(4),... prime(N)`. These prime candidates react with each other such that each number absorbs multiples of itself, so that only prime numbers remain in the end. One sample computation is

```
prime(7),prime(6),prime(5),prime(4),prime(3),prime(2) ↦
prime(7),  prime(5),  prime(4),  prime(3),  prime(2) ↦
prime(7),  prime(5),  prime(3),  prime(2)
```

Example 6.1.3 (Destructive Assignment) Declarative programs come with the property of *immutability*. It means that variables cannot be updated and that data structures cannot be modified in-place. Instead, new data structures must be created to reflect the change, so updates may be more costly. The advantage is that immutability makes the program's behavior more predictable and facilitates concurrent execution. Declarative programs are thus easier to reason about and debug than imperative languages.

In declarative CHR it is possible to efficiently simulate *destructive (multiple) assignment* of imperative programming languages. We store variable names and their value in the CHR constraint `cell/2` and use the CHR constraint `assign/2` to assign a new value to a variable:

```
assign(Var,New), cell(Var,Old) <=> cell(Var,New).
```

An optimizing CHR compiler can translate this type of recursion into in-place updates in the implementation language. This means that destructive assignment can be simulated in constant time. This is not known to be possible in other pure declarative languages and a source of the effectiveness of CHR.

Note that the rule is not confluent. The critical state `cell(X,A)`, `assign(X,B)`, `assign(X,C)` leads to the non-joinable critical pair `cell(X,B) <> cell(X,C)`. The confluence analysis shows that the order of the updates matters. This gives the core reason why imperative languages are hard to analyse and hard to parallelize.

6.2 Top-Down Evaluation

As we will see with the example of *Fibonacci numbers*, in CHR it is easy to change between different evaluation methods.

Example 6.2.1 (Fibonacci Numbers, Definition) The Fibonacci number function is defined inductively as follows:

$$fib(0) = fib(1) = 1 \text{ and } fib(n) = fib(n-1) + fib(n-2) \text{ for } n \geq 2$$

When we implement this definition in CHR, we translate the functional notation of fib into a relational notation, and the equivalence becomes a simplification rule. The CHR constraint `fib(N,M)` holds if the N-th Fibonacci number is M.

We first employ a more traditional style of programming, where constraints resemble procedures in imperative programming languages. Results of a computation are not returned as constraints, but as values of variables that become *bound*. This approach of reasoning and programming starts with a problem and breaks it down in smaller and smaller subproblems. *Top-down evaluation* is also called *goal-driven evaluation* and *backward chaining*.

Example 6.2.2 (Fibonacci Numbers, Top-Down) For our problem, top-down evaluation results in a recursive approach where we start from the highest Fibonacci number.

```
f0 @ fib(0,M) <=> M=1.
f1 @ fib(1,M) <=> M=1.
fn @ fib(N,M) <=> N>=2 |
            fib(N-1,M1), fib(N-2,M2), M is M1+M2.
```

The rules are a direct translation of the definition into relational notation. In the concrete Prolog syntax of CHR, we use the symbol @ instead of : after rule identifiers. As is well known, such a direct implementation has exponential time complexity because of the double recursion that recomputes the same Fibonacci numbers again and again.

6.2.1 Memoization

For efficiency, we would like to store and reuse solutions to subproblems that we already have computed. This approach is called *memoization (memoring)* or *tabulation (tabling)*. Since CHR constraints are both operations and data, it is easy to change the rules accordingly.

Example 6.2.3 (Fibonacci Numbers, Memoization) We just turn the three simplification rules into propagation rules, so that the left hand side constraints are kept. In addition, we need a rule for the look-up of already computed Fibonacci numbers. This rule mem has to come first, so that it is applied before we try to compute in the usual way. It actually expresses a *functional dependency* for the constraint fib/2. As with any function, the input determines the output.

```
mem @ fib(N,M1) \ fib(N,M2) <=> M1=M2.
```

```
f0 @ fib(0,M) ==> M=1.
f1 @ fib(1,M) ==> M=1.
fn @ fib(N,M) ==> N>=2 |
            fib(N-1,M1), fib(N-2,M2), M is M1+M2.
```

Remember that in a simpagation rule, the currently active constraint matches the removable constraints first so that it is removed if possible. The query fib(8,A) now returns all Fibonacci numbers up to 8, i.e. fib(0,1), fib(1,1), fib(2,2),..., fib(7,21), fib(8,34).

The effect of memoization is dramatic: while the original rules have exponential complexity, the new version has only linear complexity, because each Fibonacci number is only computed once.

6.3 Bottom-Up Evaluation

Reasoning *bottom-up* starts from the given facts (solutions to small subproblems) and proceeds towards a solution by deriving new facts that solve larger subproblems. The approach is also called *forward chaining* and *data-driven evaluation*.

Example 6.3.1 (Fibonacci Numbers, Bottom-up) We compute larger Fibonacci numbers from smaller ones. Basically, it suffices to reverse head and body of the recursive rule for Fibonacci in rule `fn`. The computation can be made finite by introducing an upper bound `Max`. With the rules below, the query `fib_upto(Max)`, `fib(0,1)`, `fib(1,1)` will produce all Fibonacci numbers up to `Max`.

```
fn @ fib_upto(Max), fib(N1,M1), fib(N2,M2) ==>
            Max>N2, N2 is N1+1 | fib(N2+1,M1+M2).
```

When we turn the propagation rule into a simpagation rule that only keeps the last two Fibonacci numbers, the resulting program is even faster.

```
fn @ fib(Max), fib(N2,M2) \ fib(N1,M1) <=>
            Max>N2, N2 is N1+1 | fib(N2+1,M1+M2).
```

This rule is now also an example of multiset transformation.

We now embark on a different example.

Example 6.3.2 (Transitive Closure) Transitive closure is an essential operation that occurs in graph algorithms, automated reasoning and constraint solving. The transitive closure of a binary relation is the smallest transitive relation that contains it. A relation is transitive whenever it relates a to b and b to c, then it also relates a to c.

33

We can depict the relation as a *directed graph*, where there is a directed edge (arc) from node (vertex) *a* to node *b* whenever *a* relates to *b*. The transitive closure then corresponds to all paths in the graph. In CHR, we implement the given relation as graph with edge constraints e/2 and its transitive closure with path constraints p/2.

```
dp @ p(X,Y) \ p(X,Y) <=> true.
```

```
p1 @ e(X,Y) ==> p(X,Y).
pn @ e(X,Y), p(Y,Z) ==> p(X,Z).
```

The two propagation rules compute the transitive closure bottom-up. In the rule p1, for each edge, a corresponding path is added. If there is an edge from X to Y then there is also a path from X to Y. The rule pn extends an existing path with an edge in front. If there is an edge from X to Y and a path from Y to Z then there is also a path from X to Z. Termination is ensured by the simpagation rule dp which removes duplicate path constraints before they can be used. Hence the rule has to come first in the program.

For example, the evaluation of the query e(1,2), e(2,3), e(2,4) adds the path constraints p(1,2), p(2,3), p(2,4), p(1,3), p(1,4).

6.4 Exercises CHR

Exercise 1: Chemical Reaction

Water molecules result from hydrogen and oxygen when they are heated. With electricity, the water molecules can be decomposed into hydrogen and oxygen. These chemical reactions can be expressed as:

$$\text{heat} + 2H_2 + O_2 \rightarrow 2H_2O$$

$$\text{electricity} + 2H_2O \rightarrow 2H_2 + O_2$$

Use nullary CHR constraints h2, o2, h2o, heat, electricity. Assuming that one heat or electricity unit is needed for each reaction, write CHR rules to model these reactions. Test your program with queries and their expected answers such as:

34

```
heat,h2,h2,o2 ↦* h2o, h2o
heat,h2,h2,o2,h2,h2,o2 ↦* h2,h2,o2,h2o,h2o
heat,h2,h2,o2,h2,h2,o2,heat ↦* h2o,h2o,h2o,h2o
heat,h2,h2,o2,h2,h2,o2,heat,electricity ↦* h2,h2,o2,h2o,h2o
electricity,electricity,h2o,h2o,h2o,h2o ↦* h2,h2,h2,h2,o2,o2
```

Exercise 2: Production Chain

Model the following production chain in the given order with rules in CHR:

- A woodcutter cuts one tree into two logs.

- In the sawmill, one log can be cut into a three boards, as well as two pieces of scrap wood.

- From three boards and one piece of scrap wood, a carpenter produces a wooden chest, as well as another piece of scrap wood.

- From a piece of scrap wood, a carver carves wooden dishes.

The resources are represented by the nullary CHR constraints `tree`, `log`, `board`, `chest`, and `dishes`. The input is any number of the above constraints. A simple example is:
`tree ↦* chest,chest, dishes,dishes,dishes,dishes`.

Keep track of how many tasks were executed. Extend your program with a constraint `tasks_executed/1`, which holds the total number of executed tasks. In the above query, the constraint `tasks_executed(9)` should also be in the answer.

Exercise 3: Levenshtein Distance

Write a CHR program that calculates the Levenshtein edit distance between two strings. The *Levenshtein* distance is the minimal number of insertion, deletion or exchange operations that are necessary to transform one string into another. The Levenshtein distance

$ldist(\alpha, \beta)$ between two strings α and ϵ is defined as follows:

$$ldist(\alpha, \epsilon) = |\alpha|$$
$$ldist(\epsilon, \beta) = |\beta|$$
$$ldist(x\alpha, y\beta) = ldist(\alpha, \beta), \qquad\qquad\qquad x = y$$
$$ldist(x\alpha, y\beta) = 1 + \min\left\{ldist(\alpha, y\beta), ldist(x\alpha, \beta), ldist(\alpha, \beta)\right\}, \quad x \neq y$$

where ϵ denotes the empty string, the function $|.|$ the length of a string and x and y are the first symbols of a string.

Use a CHR constraint `ldist/3` with the first and second argument being the input strings represented as Prolog lists and the third argument the calculated distance. Implement a rule for each of the four equations.

Improve the implementation using memoization for `ldist/3` like in the Fibonacci numbers example: Add a rule that removes `ldist/3` constraints whose input strings are the same and equates their output arguments.

Selected Solutions

Production Chain

```
woodcutter @ tree <=>
    log, log,
    tasks_executed(1).

sawmill @ log <=>
    board, board, board, scrapwood, scrapwood,
    tasks_executed(1).

carpenter @ board, board, board, scrapwood <=>
    chest, scrapwood,
    tasks_executed(1).

carver @ scrapwood <=>
    dishes,
    tasks_executed(1).
```

```
accumulate @ tasks_executed(N), tasks_executed(M) <=>
   S is N + M, tasks_executed(S).
```

Levenshtein Distance

```
% memoization
ldist(Xs,Ys,ED1) \ ldist(Xs,Ys,ED2) <=> ED1 = ED2.

% equation 1
ldist([],Ys,LD) ==> length(Ys,LD).

% equation 2
ldist(Xs,[],LD) ==> length(Xs,LD).

% equation 3
ldist([X|Xs],[X|Ys],LD) ==> ldist(Xs,Ys,LD).

% equation 4
ldist([X|Xs],[Y|Ys],LD) ==> X \= Y |
    ldist([X|Xs],Ys,LD1),
    ldist(Xs,[Y|Ys],LD2),
    ldist(Xs,Ys,LD3),
    LD is 1 + min(LD1,min(LD2,LD3)).
```

Chapter 7

Pragmatics of Embeddings into CHR

For the embedding of rule-based approaches in CHR it is often sufficient to use a syntactic subset of CHR. In *positive ground range-restricted (PGR)* CHR, queries are ground and rules are restricted to be positive and range-restricted. *Positive* means that there are no built-in constraints in the body of rules except *true*. This means that computations cannot fail because inconsistent built-in constraints cannot arise. *Range-restricted* means that the rules have no local variables, i.e. every variable from the guard and body also occurs in the rule head. For practical reasons, the condition of range restriction can and will be relaxed. We allow auxiliary functions that are expressed as built-in constraints with local variables in the rule body if their results can be computed whenever the variables in the head are ground. Finally, queries are assumed to be *ground*. As a consequence of range-restrictedness, every state in the computation will be ground.

For the embeddings, we will translate each rule of our chosen rule-based approach to one or more CHR rules according to a *rule scheme*. For more advanced embeddings, we will also need some *helper rules* that are not the result of a rule translation, but implement additional functionality needed to embed the approach at hand. For examples, we will continue to use the concrete syntax of CHR in the host language Prolog.

CHR in SWI-Prolog is online with dozens of example programs at `https://chr.informatik.uni-ulm.de/swish/` and SWI-Prolog can be downloaded for free at `https://www.swi-prolog.org/`. Examples involving constants only also run with minor modification in the Javascript implementation of CHR at `http://chrjs.net/`. Many CHR implementations can be found online on coding platforms like `Github`.

Part II

RULE-BASED FORMALISMS

Rule-based formalisms are usually considered as a theoretical means and are rarely directly implemented as a programming language. Still, CHR can express and execute the essential aspects of these formalisms. For the embeddings in CHR, states in the original computational formalism are mapped to CHR constraints, and transitions are mapped to CHR rules. This allows for the high-level implementation of the original formalism in CHR.

We will introduce embeddings of the following rule-based formalisms into CHR:

- General Abstract Model for Multiset Manipulation (GAMMA) is a computational model for transforming a multiset of data as specified by mapping functions which can be considered as implicit rewrite rules.

- Petri Nets (PN) are a graph-based diagrammatic formalism to describe and analyze the behavior of concurrent and distributed systems. Computation is performed by tokens moving along arcs and residing at nodes.

- Term Rewriting Systems (TRS) are a formalism that uses directed equations as rewrite rules to replace subterms in a given term.

- Functional Programming (FP) is a declarative programming paradigm based on mathematical functions defined by directed equations. FP is related to TRS and therefore presented in this part.

Chapter 8

General Abstract Model for Multiset Manipulation (GAMMA)

General Abstract Model for Multiset Manipulation (GAMMA) [9, 10] uses a chemical metaphor. It regards states as chemical solutions containing molecules that can react with each other. These reactions can operate concurrently and can change, delete, or create molecules. GAMMA is the basis of the Chemical Abstract Machine (CHAM) [13].

8.1 GAMMA Syntax and Semantics

GAMMA executes by repeatedly applying the reaction rules to the molecules until no more reactions are possible. The result of the execution is the final set of molecules.

Def. 8.1.1 (GAMMA Syntax and Semantics) Given a set D of *molecules (data elements)*, a GAMMA program consists of *GAMMA pairs (reactions)* $p = (c/n, f/n)$ with a name p, an n-ary condition c over n molecules of D and an n-ary function $f : D^n \to 2^D$.

Given a multiset $S = \{x_1, \ldots, x_n\} \cup S'$ the transition $\mapsto_p$ for a

GAMMA pair $p = (c/n, f/n)$ is defined as

$$\{x_1, \ldots, x_n\} \cup S' \mapsto_p \{y_1, \ldots, y_m\} \cup S'$$
$$\text{if } c(x_1, \ldots, x_n) \text{ and } f(x_1, \ldots, x_n) = \{y_1, \ldots, y_m\}.$$

A computation starts from an *initial multiset* and ends if no more transition is possible. ■

Given a multiset S of molecules on which to operate, the function f/n can be applied to a subset of n molecules of S, if c/n holds for them. The result of the function will replace these molecules.

8.2 Embedding GAMMA in CHR

In the embedding, molecules are wrapped by unary CHR constraints and GAMMA pairs are mapped to simplification rules. The translation of a GAMMA pair encodes the condition as guard and the function as built-in or CHR constraint in the rule body.

Def. 8.2.1 (Rule Scheme for GAMMA) A GAMMA pair $p = (c/n, f/n)$ is translated to CHR simplification rule

$$p \ @ \ d(x_1), \ldots, d(x_n) \Leftrightarrow c(x_1, \ldots, x_n) \ | \ f(x_1, \ldots, x_n),$$

where the CHR constraint $d/1$ wraps molecules, c/n is a built-in constraint, and the CHR constraint f/n is defined by one or more rules of the form

$$f(x_1, \ldots, x_n) \Leftrightarrow C \ | \ D, d(y_1), \ldots, d(y_m),$$

where C is a guard and D are auxiliary constraints.

The initial multiset $S = \{z_1, \ldots, z_k\}$ is translated to a CHR query $d(z_1), \ldots, d(z_k)$. ■

Note by abuse of notation, the function f/n becomes a relation as CHR constraint that is directly replaced by the resulting molecules.

46

Examples GAMMA in CHR

The examples illustrate how GAMMA encodes multiset rewriting. In each example code, the first line specifies a given GAMMA pair, which consists of a name, a condition and a function. The corresponding CHR rules are the translation of these GAMMA pairs.

Example 8.2.1 (Minimum in GAMMA) The GAMMA program computes the minimum of a set of numbers.

```
% GAMMA pair min = (</2,first/2)
min @ d(X), d(Y) <=> X<Y | first(X,Y).
     first(X,Y) <=> d(X).
```

It defines a pair called min with a condition that checks if the first number X is less than the second number Y and a function that returns the first number. So in effect the second, larger number is removed. Different to the rule for the minimum example from the CHR introduction, duplicates of the minimum numbers remain.

Example 8.2.2 (Prime Sieve in GAMMA) The GAMMA pair sieves a set of numbers from 1 to some upper bound so that only primes remain. If X divides Y, the function removes Y and returns X. In this way, all multiples of a number are removed and only prime numbers remain. The behavior of the rules is the same as in the primes example from the CHR introduction.

```
% GAMMA pair prime = (div/2,first/2)
prime @ d(X), d(Y) <=> X div Y | first(X,Y).
        first(X,Y) <=> d(X).
```

Example 8.2.3 (Greatest Common Divisor in GAMMA) The GAMMA pair reduces the problem of finding the gcd of X and Y to finding the gcd of X and Y-X. The computation terminates when the guard condition X<Y is no longer satisfied, at which point X and Y are the same value and the GCD is simply X itself.

```
% GAMMA pair gcd = (</2,gcdsub/2)
gcd @ d(X), d(Y) <=> X<Y | gcdsub(X,Y).
      gcdsub(X,Y) <=> d(X), d(Y-X).
```

We show now how *partial evaluation* can be applied to rules resulting from the GAMMA embedding in CHR.

Example 8.2.4 (Partial Evaluation of GAMMA in CHR)
For partial evaluation of the rule gcd, we execute its guard and body X<Y, gcdsub(X,Y) and replace the body with the resulting constraints d(X), d(Y-X). Since d(X) occurs both in the head and body now, the rule can be represented as a CHR simpagation rule

gcd @ d(X) \ d(Y) <=> X<Y | d(Y-X).

This rule is basically the one from the GCD Example 6.1.1 in the CHR introduction. The partial evaluation of the rule removes the constraint gcdsub(X, Y), it is no longer needed for the computation of the gcd. Thus the rule defining it can also be removed.

8.3 Embedding Gamma (γ) Abstraction in CHR

GAMMA with γ-abstraction is an extension of the GAMMA computational model which introduces variables. It allows for the definition of anonymous, nameless functions.

Def. 8.3.1 (Rule Scheme for GAMMA with γ-Abstraction)
A given GAMMA pair with γ-abstraction

$$g = (\gamma(x_1, \ldots, x_n) : C, (f_1(\bar{x}_1), \ldots, f_m(\bar{x}_m)))$$

where C is a condition on the molecules $x_1, \ldots, x_n$ and $f_1, \ldots, f_m$ are functions applied to molecules from $x_1, \ldots, x_n$ that return a single molecule, is translated to the CHR PGR simplification rule

$$g@d(x_1), \ldots, d(x_n) \Leftrightarrow C \mid f_1(\bar{x}_1, y_1), \ldots, f_m(\bar{x}_m, y_m), d(y_1), \ldots, d(y_m)$$

where the f_i are built-in constraints or CHR constraints defined by PGR simplification rules of the form

$$f_i(\bar{x}_i, y_i) \Leftrightarrow C_i \mid D_i,$$

where C_i is a guard and D_i is a body computing y_i from $\bar{x}_i$. ∎

In this embedding, a function f/n is represented by a relation $f/n+1$ where the added last argument is the result of the function.

Examples GAMMA with γ-Abstraction in CHR

We redo the previous examples using γ-abstraction. The resulting code now uses variables and is closer to its CHR translation. Some code is more concise because functions like `first/2` or identity are not needed when using variables. We express such functions simply by mentioning the variable.

Example 8.3.1 (Minimum, GCD, Prime Sieve) Our running examples can now be written as follows.

```
% GAMMA min = ([X,Y]:X<Y,[X])
min @ d(X), d(Y) <=> X<Y | d(X).


% GAMMA gcd = ([X,Y]:X<Y,[X,Y-X])
gcd @ d(X), d(Y) <=> X<Y | d(X), d(Y-X).


% GAMMA prime = ([X,Y]:X div Y,[X])
prime @ d(X), d(Y) <=> X div Y | d(X).
```

8.4 Embedding CHR Subset in GAMMA

GAMMA can embed CHR PGR simplification rules when CHR constraints of arbitrary arity $c(\bar{z})$ are represented as terms in the argument of the unary constraint $d(c(\bar{z}))$. This makes GAMMA equivalent to the PGR simplification and simpagation rule subset of CHR, because CHR propagation rules cannot be embedded in this way since they would cause nontermination. The translation is basically the inversion on the rule level of the embedding of GAMMA in CHR.

Def. 8.4.1 (CHR Subset in GAMMA with γ-Abstraction) A CHR generalized PGR simplification rule of the form

$$r \ @ \ c_1(\bar{x}_1), \ldots, c_n(\bar{x}_n) \Leftrightarrow c(\bar{x}_1, \ldots, \bar{x}_n) \mid D, c'_1(\bar{y}_1), \ldots, c'_m(\bar{y}_m),$$

where the $y_1, \ldots, y_m$ are local variables, the $\bar{y}_1, \ldots, \bar{y}_m$ do not contain new variables, and D is a goal, is translated to a GAMMA pair with

γ-abstraction

$$r = (\gamma(v_1, \ldots, v_n) : (v_1{=}c_1(\bar{x}_1) \wedge \ldots v_n{=}c_n(\bar{x}_n) \wedge c(\bar{x}_1, \ldots, \bar{x}_n)),$$
$$(f_1(\ldots), \ldots, f_m(\ldots)))$$

where $f_1, \ldots, f_m$ are functions applied to molecules from $v_1, \ldots, v_n$ that implement the computations from D such that $f_i(\ldots) = d(c'_i(\bar{y}_i))$.
∎

Example 8.4.1 (Destructive Assignment in GAMMA)   The CHR rule for destructive assignment from Example 6.1.3 can be expressed in GAMMA with γ-abstraction as follows.

```
% CHR rule
assign(Var,New), cell(Var,Old) <=> cell(Var,New).

% GAMMA pair
assign = ([A,B]:(A=assign(Var,New),B=cell(Var,_)),
                [cell(Var,New)])
```

where the underscore symbol _ denotes a *anonymous (unnamed) variable*, i.e. a variable whose value is not of interest.

8.5 Exercises GAMMA

Exercise 4: Chemical Reaction Rules to GAMMA

Recall the chemical reactions from Exercise 6.4:

$$\text{heat} + 2H_2 + O_2 \rightarrow 2H_2O$$

$$\text{electricity} + 2H_2O \rightarrow 2H_2 + O_2$$

Translate this chemical reaction rules into GAMMA.

Exercise 5: Fibonacci Numbers in GAMMA

Define the computation of Fibonacci numbers in GAMMA and in GAMMA with γ-abstraction.

Chapter 9

Colored Petri Nets (CPN)

Graph-based diagrammatic formalisms like Petri Nets, Statecharts and UML Activity Diagrams describe activities and processes by moving control and data tokens along arcs in a graph. The diagrams implicitly define rewrite rules for tokens. Petri Nets [58] model the behavior of distributed and concurrent systems in a formal way for analysis, including communication protocols, manufacturing processes, and biological systems. Petri Nets and Colored Petri Nets are translated to CHR in [15].

9.1 PN Syntax and Semantics

The graph of a Petri Net has two disjoint sets of nodes, places and transitions. The edges of the graph are directed and go from places to transitions or vice versa. These arcs represent the flow of tokens in the Petri Net. Each place may be empty or hold a finite number of tokens.

Def. 9.1.1 (PN Syntax) A *Petri Net (PN)* is defined as a triple (P, T, F), where P is a finite set of *places*, T is a finite set of *transitions*, and $F \subseteq (P \times T) \cup (T \times P)$ is a finite multiset of *arcs* connecting places to transitions and transitions to places.

Petri Nets are drawn as diagrams, where places are circles containing dots as tokens, transitions are rectangles and arcs are straight lines between places and transitions. ∎

Tokens can move along arcs passing through transitions from one place to another. A transition may have several incoming and several outgoing arcs. A transition can only fire if all incoming arcs present tokens. On firing, one token from each incoming arc will be removed and one token will be presented on each outgoing arc and added to the corresponding places.

Def. 9.1.2 (PN Semantics) Given a PN, *states* are multisets of places from P which are interpreted as tokens in those places. A transition is *enabled* if the places of each incoming arc contain at least one token. *Firing* an enabled transition means removing one token from each place and adding one token to each place of the outgoing arcs. A *run* of a PN is any sequence of firings. ∎

Even though computations of a Petri Net are often infinite, there are several analysis problems that are decidable for Petri Nets, for example freeness of deadlocks. Deadlocks refer to states in which no progress can be made because no transition is enabled.

9.2 Embedding PN in CHR

A small fragment of CHR can encode the behavior of a Petri Net. A token at a place corresponds to a constraint, and all places involved in a transition constitute a rule. Specifically, nullary CHR constraints represent a token at a place and PGR simplification rules without guards and without built-ins represent transitions between these places.

Def. 9.2.1 (Rule Scheme for PN) For each place $p_i \in P$ we introduce a CHR token constraint `pi`. A PN state is represented in CHR as a conjunction of token constraints. For each transition $t_i \in T$ we introduce a CHR simplification rule named `ti`, whose head is the conjunction of all places p_j where $(p_j, t_i) \in F$ and whose body is the conjunction of all places p_k where $(t_i, p_k) \in F$. ∎

Example PN in CHR

Example 9.2.1 (Petri Net) In Figure 9.1, places are drawn as circles, transitions are drawn as rectangles and tokens as black dots. The

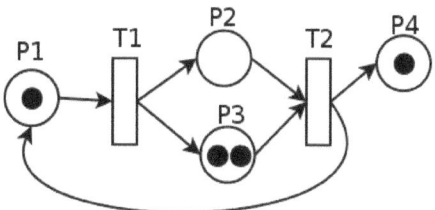

Figure 9.1: A Petri Net Example

PN is translated into the following PGR simplification rules in CHR:

```
t1 @ p1 <=> p2, p3
t2 @ p2, p3 <=> p1, p4
```

The constraints p1, p2, p3, and p4 represent tokens at places, and the rules t1 and t2 represent transitions between places. The first rule, t1 @ p1 <= p2, p3, states that if the token at p1 is present, it can be removed and the tokens at p2 and p3 should be added to the goal. This corresponds to the behavior of transition T1 in the PN, which consumes one token from place p1 and produces two tokens in places p2 and p3. Similarly, the second rule, t2 @ p2, p3 <= p1, p4, states that if the tokens at p2 and p3 are present, they can be replaced by the tokens at p1 and p4. This corresponds to the behavior of transition T2 in the PN.

The state of the PN in the figure corresponds to the CHR state p1,p3,p3,p4. Executing it as a query leads to the firing of rule t1 with p1 and then rule t2, resulting in the intermediate state p1,p4,p3,p3,p4. It is easy to see that the computation will not terminate and increase the number of p4 tokens only.

9.3 Colored Petri Nets (CPN)

We consider a generalization of PN, *Colored Petri Nets (CPN)*. In CPN, tokens that flow through the net have different colors (values). This allows for type constraints to be placed on places to only allow

53

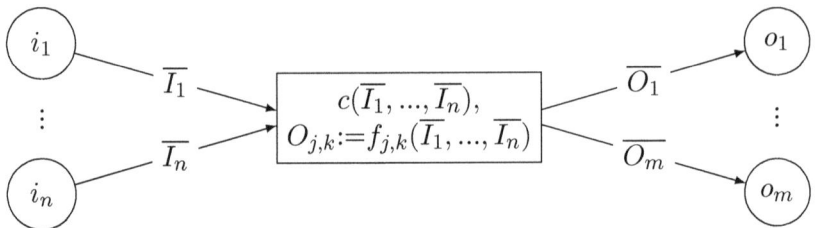

Figure 9.2: CPN Transition

certain colors of tokens. Transitions in CPN are guarded by conditions that are evaluated based on the colors of the incoming tokens. If the conditions are satisfied, the transition is enabled. On firing, new tokens are generated by equations which are also given in the transition. The decidability of properties of CPNs depends on the specific properties of the CPN being considered.

9.4 Embedding CPN in CHR

Consider an arbitrary CPN transition with its incoming and outgoing arcs as given in Figure 9.2. The i_i and o_j are the names of the places, the $\overline{I_i}$ and $\overline{O_j}$ are the token variables along the arcs, c is a condition on the incoming tokens, and $O_{j,k}$ are the variables for the resulting outgoing tokens produced by applying functions $f_{j,k}$ to incoming tokens.

When translated to CHR, places are represented by unary CHR constraints named by places and with the arguments representing the tokens. Transitions are represented by PGR simplification rules with the places of the incoming arcs forming the rule head, the transition condition as the rule guard, and the transition equation and places of the outgoing arcs forming the rule body.

Def. 9.4.1 (Rule Scheme for CPN) Each transition of the a CPN

54

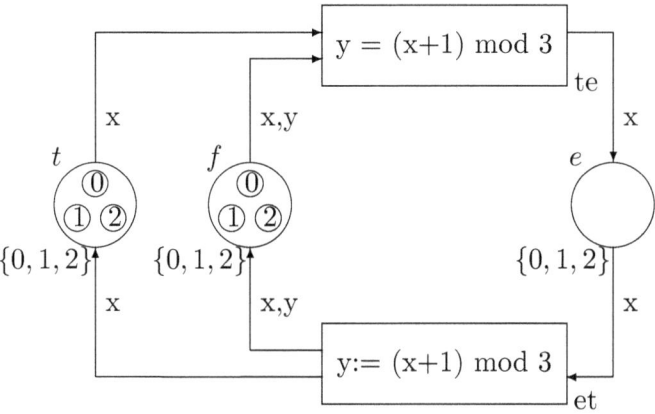

Figure 9.3: CPN for Three Dining Philosophers Problem

(Figure 9.2) translates to a PGR simplification rule

$$i_1(I_{1,1}), \ldots, i_1(I_{1,l_1}), \ldots, i_n(I_{n,1}), \ldots, i_n(I_{n,l_n}) \Leftrightarrow c(\overline{I_1}, \ldots, \overline{I_n}) \mid$$
$$f_{1,1}(\overline{I_1}, \ldots, \overline{I_n}, O_{1,1}), \ldots, f_{1,l_1'}(\overline{I_1}, \ldots, \overline{I_n}, O_{1,l_1'}), \ldots,$$
$$f_{m,1}(\overline{I_1}, \ldots, \overline{I_n}, O_{m,1}), \ldots, f_{m,l_m'}(\overline{I_1}, \ldots, \overline{I_n}, O_{m,l_m'}),$$
$$o_1(O_{1,1}), \ldots, o_1(O_{1,l_1'}), \ldots, o_m(O_{m,1}), \ldots, o_m(O_{m,l_m'}),$$

where $\overline{I_i} = I_{i,1}, \ldots, I_{i,l_i}$ and $\overline{O_i} = O_{i,1}, \ldots, O_{i,l_i'}$. ∎

Example Dining Philosophers in CPN and CHR

The dining philosophers problem is a classic example in computer science that introduces the concept of fairness. It illustrates the challenges of resource allocation and synchronization in a concurrent environment. A number of philosophers sit at a round table. Between each philosopher a fork is placed. A philosopher either thinks or eats. In order to eat, a philosopher needs two forks, the one from his left and the one from his right. After a while, an eating philosopher will start to think again, releasing both forks and thus making them available to his neighbors again. Without fairness, it is possible for some philosophers to always eat while others starve, leading to an unfair distribution of resources. The problem is to design a protocol that ensures that the philosophers can eat their meals without getting stuck in a deadlock or a starvation situation.

When the problem is modeled as a standard PN, we need places and transitions for the behavior of each philosopher separately. In the CPN formulation (Figure 9.3), places and transitions are generic for any philosopher. However, the number of philosophers still has to be fixed, here it is three. Each philosopher corresponds to a colored token (a number $0, 1$ or 2). Two tokens x and y representing philosophers are neighbors if the transition guard $(y = (x+1) \mod 3)$ holds. There are three places in the CPN: one for eating (e), one for thinking (t), and one for the forks (f). Transitions go from eat to think (et) and from think to eat (te). Transition et has no guard but an equation that produces an additional token y representing a fork. Initially, all philosophers think, and thus all forks are available.

CPN Dining Philosophers in CHR   The Three Dining Philosophers CPN is encoded in CHR by the following two PGR simplification rules:

```
te @ t(X),f(X),f(Y) <=> Y is (X+1) mod 3 | e(X).
et @ e(X) <=> Y is (X+1) mod 3, t(X),f(X),f(Y).
```

The rule te has the head constraints t(X) and f(X), f(Y). The first constraint represents a thinking philosopher t(X) who is trying to eat, and the remaining constraints represent the availability of the forks on the left and right of the philosopher. The rule body consists of a single constraint e(X). This constraint represents the philosopher who is eating. The rule et enables a philosopher to finish eating. Note that the et rule is the reverse of the te rule, it allows for the reverse transition from eating to thinking. Note that the execution in CHR is not fair. Fairness can be achieved using conflict resolution (cf. Section 12.4). The number of philosophers can be made a parameter in the CHR rules, while it is fixed in the CPN model. This means that the CHR rules can model any given number of philosophers.

9.5 Comparison GAMMA, CPN and CHR

CPN use a diagrammatic notation to describe the movement of tokens in a graph, while GAMMA uses condition-function pairs to describe reactions of molecules in a chemical solution. The embeddings of GAMMA and CPN result in specific syntactic subsets of PGR simplification rules of CHR.

We compare their rule schemes with PGR simplification rules. The main syntactical difference between GAMMA, CPN, and PGR subset of CHR is in the arity of CHR constraints. Translated GAMMA and CPN rules can only handle unary CHR constraints and constraints representing functions. CPN generalizes GAMMA by allowing arbitrary unary constraints instead of just $d/1$. Still, as we have seen, GAMMA, CPN and PGR CHR simplification rules are equally expressive because the can be embedded into each other.

The embedding of CPN in CHR allows for cross-fertilization between the approaches, in particular concerning analysis. For example, one could apply deadlock analysis of CPN to GAMMA and the PGR subset of CHR. Another example is the use of confluence analysis of CHR to analyze the fairness of CPN and GAMMA.

Embedding CHR Subset in CPN Like GAMMA, CPN can embed generalized CHR PGR simplification rules [15] with the exception of propagation rules when CHR constraints of arbitrary arity $c(\bar{z})$ are represented as terms in the argument of the unary constraint $d(c(\bar{z}))$. Since the embedding is as expressive as for GAMMA, CPN and GAMMA are equivalent as well. As a consequence, both GAMMA and generalized CHR PGR simplification rules can be drawn as CPN.

9.6 Exercises CPN

Exercise 6: CHR to PN

Recall the wood-processing CHR program from Exercise 6.4. Translate this program into a Petri Net, i.e., draw the corresponding graph.

Exercise 7: CHR to CPN

Recall the GCD CHR program. Translate this program into a CPN diagram.

Chapter 10

Term Rewriting Systems (TRS)

Term Rewriting Systems (TRS) [8] manipulate a term by applying rewrite rules to its subterms. Typical applications of TRS languages are theorem proving and modeling.

10.1 TRS Syntax and Semantics

Term Rewriting Systems (TRS) are formally based on equational logic, which deals with the theory of equations. An equation is a statement of equality between two expressions. In TRS, the equations become directed, they are read from left to right as rewrite rules.

Def. 10.1.1 (TRS Syntax) A *Term Rewriting System (TRS)* is a set of rewrite rules of the form $l \rightarrow r$, where l and r are terms. The rewrite rules are range-restricted and linear. *Range-restricted* means that the variables of the right-hand side (RHS) also occur in the left-hand side (LHS) of the rule. *Linear* means that the variables in the LHS are all distinct and that the variables in the RHS are all distinct.
∎

In a TRS, rewrite rules are applied to a term to reduce it. The application of a rule to a term is called a rewriting step or reduction. The left-hand side of a rule is called a pattern. If a subterm of the term matches the pattern, the right-hand side of the rule under this matching is used to replace the matching subterm.

Def. 10.1.2 (TRS Operational Semantics) Given a rule $s \to t$ and a ground term u with a subterm v at position p that matches s with substitution β, a *rewriting step (reduction, transition)* of a TRS is defined as follows:

$$u[v]_p \mapsto u[t\beta]_p \text{ if } v = s\beta \text{ and } s \to t.$$

A *TRS computation* is a sequence of reduction steps starting from an *initial ground term*. A term t is said to be *in normal form* if no rule is applicable to any of its subterms. ∎

In the reduction, we replace v by t under substitution β at position p in u. Note that the subterm v may be the term u itself. The normal form may not be unique because different rule applications can lead to different terms. If a TRS does not have a normal form, it is not terminating.

The declarative semantics of TRS interprets TRS rules as axiom formulas in equational logic.

Def. 10.1.3 (TRS Declarative Semantics) A TRS rule $s \to t$ is interpreted as axiom formula $\forall s = t$, where $=$ is an equality relation over terms. The equality relation is reflexive, symmetric, transitive, but also satisfies

$$f(X_1, \ldots, X_n) = g(Y_1, \ldots, Y_m) \Leftrightarrow f \doteq g \wedge n \doteq m \wedge X_1 = Y_1 \wedge \ldots \wedge X_n = Y_m,$$

where $\doteq$ is the syntactic identity relation. ∎

10.2 Embedding TRS in CHR

The key idea behind the embedding is to translate each TRS rule into a CHR simplification rule over equality constraints as prescribed by the declarative semantics of a TRS [61].

Term Flattening For the embedding of TRS (and later functional programs) in CHR, we need the notion of term flattening. A term is *flat* if it is a variable or if its arguments are variables, otherwise it is *nested*, i.e. it has subterms that are not variables. A term can be *flattened* by replacing each subterm with a new variable that is equated with the replaced subterm.

Def. 10.2.1 (Flattening) The *flattening function* $\downarrow$ transforms an equality constraint X eq t, where X is a variable and t is a term, into a conjunction of flat equations as follows:

$$\downarrow(X \text{ eq } t) :=$$

$$\begin{cases} X \text{ eq } t & \text{if } t \text{ is a variable} \\ X \text{ eq } f(X_1, \ldots, X_n) \wedge \bigwedge_{i=1}^{n} \downarrow(X_i \text{ eq } t_i) & \text{if } t = f(t_1, \ldots, t_n) \end{cases}$$

where $X_1, \ldots, X_n$ are new distinct variables. ∎

Flattening increases the size of an equality by a constant factor, since we introduce a variable and a flat equation for each subterm in the equation.

TRS in CHR To embed TRS into CHR, the declarative semantics of TRS is utilized. Each TRS rule $s \rightarrow t$ is interpreted as an axiom formula $\forall(X \text{ eq } s \Leftrightarrow X \text{ eq } t)$ and mapped to a simplification rule for equality constraints with the help of the flattening function.

Def. 10.2.2 (Rule Scheme for TRS) Let eq be a binary CHR constraint denoting equality written in infix notation. A TRS rule

$$s \rightarrow t$$

translates to a CHR simplification rule

$$\downarrow(X \text{ eq } s) \Leftrightarrow \downarrow(X \text{ eq } t),$$

where X is a new variable.

An initial TRS term t is translated to a CHR query $\downarrow(X \text{ eq } t)$. ∎

Note that the resulting CHR simplification rules are not range-restricted due to the introduction of new variables during flattening.

Examples TRS in CHR

Consider the following examples for translating TRS into CHR.

Example 10.2.1 (Addition of Natural Numbers) The two re-write rules define the addition of natural numbers in successor notation:

```
0+Y -> Y.
s(X)+Y -> s(X+Y).
```

The first rule says that when we add 0 to any natural number Y, the result is Y. The second rule says that when we add the successor of a natural number X (denoted by s(X)) to another natural number Y, the result is the successor of the sum of X and Y, i.e. s(X+Y). The embedding into CHR with the help of flattening results in these two simplification rules:

```
T eq T1+T2, T1 eq 0, T2 eq Y <=> T eq Y.
T eq T1+T2, T1 eq s(T3), T3 eq X, T2 eq Y <=>
              T eq s(T4), T4 eq T5+T6, T5 eq X, T6 eq Y.
```

Example 10.2.2 (Boolean Conjunction) Here is a simple TRS for conjunction in propositional logic (Boolean Algebra). In the code, X and Y are propositional variables. The constant 0 stands for false and 1 for true. The term and(X,Y) stands for X∧Y.

```
and(0,Y) -> 0.
and(1,Y) -> Y.
```

The first TRS rule says that if the first argument of the conjunction is false, then the result will also be false. The second rule says that if the first argument is true and the other is some value, the result will be that value. The embedding into CHR yields:

```
T eq and(T1,T2), T1 eq 0, T2 eq Y <=> T eq 0.
T eq and(T1,T2), T1 eq 1, T2 eq Y <=> T eq Y.
```

Note that the CHR translation also works for non-ground queries, while TRS only work for ground queries. For example the term and(1,A) is not reducible in a TRS because it contains a variable. The CHR translation T eq and(T1,T2), T1 eq 1, T2 eq A can be rewritten with the second rule and yields the correct answer T eq A.

10.3 Embedding CHR Subset in TRS

We can translate a subset of CHR simplification rules without built-in constraints into a TRS. We try to map the CHR constraints into equations of the proper form in order to be able to reverse the flattening. We use the following algorithm.

Def. 10.3.1 (Algorithm for CHR Subset in TRS) For each CHR constraint c/n in the given CHR program choose an argument position $i(1 \leq i \leq n)$. If the program contains a nullary constraint, halt the algorithm with failure. Otherwise take such a configuration of argument positions and make an attempt to make the following transformation:

- Replace each occurrence of a constraint $c(t_1, \ldots t_n)$ in the program by an equation t_i *eq* $c(t_1, \ldots t_{i-1}, t_{i+1}, \ldots t_n)$. In the equation, we call t_i *output variable*. If t_i is not a variable, terminate the current attempt with failure.

- For each resulting rule, check if the output variables of the equations are all different except for one output variable that occurs once in the head and once in the body of the rule. This variable is called the *root*. If this is not the case, terminate the current attempt with failure.

- For each equation v *eq* t in a rule where v is not the root variable, replace all other occurrences of the output variable v by t and remove the equation. Each equation must cause a finite positive number of replacements on one side of the rule only. Otherwise terminate the current attempt with failure.

- Replace the resulting rule v *eq* $s \Leftrightarrow v$ *eq* t, where v is the root variable, by the TRS rule $s \rightarrow t$.

Queries are translated like one side of a rule (the root variable only has one occurrence then). ∎

Example 10.3.1 (Destructive Assignment in TRS) The CHR rule for destructive assignment from Example 6.1.3

63

```
assign(Var,New), cell(Var,Old) <=> cell(Var,New).
```

cannot be embedded in TRS. The only candidate for the root variable
is New because it is the only variable that occurs once on the left-
hand-side and once on the right-hand-side of the rule. This fixes the
equation representation of both constraints assign/2 and cell/2.
But the resulting rule

```
New eq assign(Var), Old eq cell(Var) <=> New eq cell(Var).
```

cannot be written as a TRS rule, because the output variable Old does
not participate in a replacement.

10.4 Comparison TRS and CHR

A Term rewriting system (TRS) is a set of rewrite rules that allow
for the replacement of terms. TRS map to simplification CHR rules
without built-ins involving only the binary CHR constraint for equality. A subset of CHR simplification rules without built-ins and with
restrictions on CHR constraint arguments can be mapped to TRS.

Both TRS and CHR programs consist of a set of rules which are
applied to specific kinds of data in order to transform them. Both
repeatedly rewrite a state until no further rule application is possible. Syntactically, TRS use a functional notation, while CHR uses
a relational notation. In TRS, rules are between terms and do not
have built-ins and guards. TRS rules also have restrictions on multiple occurrences of variables. In contrast, CHR rules are between
conjunctions of constraints and include built-ins and guards.

A TRS state is a term where all subterms have a particular fixed
position in the term, whereas a CHR state is a multiset of constraints.
While TRS rules locally rewrite subterms at fixed positions in one
ground term, CHR rules globally manipulate multiple constraints in
a multiset. During execution, TRS terms are ground, whereas CHR
constraints can contain unbound logical variables.

The language CADMIUM [22] blends CHR with term rewriting
capabilities.

10.5 Exercises TRS

Exercise 8: Multiplication and Exponentiation

Using the definition for addition with successor notation for natural numbers, implement TRS rules for multiplication and exponentiation using infix operators.

Exercise 9: Inequalities

Implement a TRS with rules for equality == and inequalities <, >, =<, >= over natural numbers in successor notation. Use the Boolean values true and false.

Selected Solutions

Multiplication and Exponentiation

```
0 * Y --> 0.
s(X) * Y --> Y + (X * Y).

_ ^ 0 --> s(0).
X ^ s(Y) --> X * (X ^ Y).
```

Inequalities

```
0 == 0 --> true.
s(_) == 0 --> false.
0 == s(_) --> false.
s(X) == s(Y) --> X == Y.

_ < 0 --> false.
0 < s(_) --> true.
s(X) < s(Y) --> X < Y.

X > Y --> Y < X.

0 =< _ --> true.
```

```
s(_) =< 0 --> false.
s(X) =< s(Y) --> X =< Y.

X >= Y --> Y =< X.
```

Chapter 11

Functional Programming (FP)

Functional Programming (FP) [51] is a declarative programming paradigm that is based on mathematical functions. These functions are pure, they do not have side-effects and their output is solely determined by their inputs. In the late 1950s, Lisp was introduced, considered by many as the first functional programming language. Modern FP languages such as Haskell [52] provide a set of constructs and idioms to support functional programming like pattern matching, higher-order functions, and algebraic data types. We will embed FP in CHR without type declarations and type checking (even though CHR has been used to advance type checking in Haskell [72]).

11.1 FP Syntax and Semantics

Functional Programming (FP) languages can be seen as based on Term Rewriting Systems (TRS). FP extends the TRS formalism by adding built-in functions and guard checks. In addition, FP introduces a clear distinction between between terms as data and as functions. To achieve this separation, FP places syntactic restrictions on the left-hand side of rewrite rules. There it disallows the nesting of functions, so functions can only be defined over data terms. A rule like `X+(Y+Z) --> (X+Y)+Z` is not allowed in FP, as the addition functions are nested. There are some exceptions to this restriction. For instance, higher-order functions are permitted, which can operate on other functions passed as arguments or return a function as a result. However, no pattern matching on functions allowed.

For FP, we extend the definitions of syntax and semantics for TRS to account for guards and built-in functions.

Def. 11.1.1 (FP Syntax) There are two disjoint sets of functions symbols to be able to distinguish two kinds of terms, *data terms* and *function calls*. Functions may be built-in or user-defined, in which case they occur on the left hand side of a rewrite rule.

A *functional program* is a set of range-restricted rewrite rules of the form $f(\bar{t}) \to G \mid s$, where $f(\bar{t})$ is a user-defined function applied to data terms $\bar{t}$, the *guard condition* G is a Boolean built-in function call and s is a data term or function call. ∎

Linearity of variable occurrences as in TRS is no longer a requirement.

Def. 11.1.2 (FP Operational Semantics) Given a ground term u with a subterm v at position p that matches s with substitution β, an *FP rewriting step (reduction, transition)* is

$$u[v]_p \mapsto u[t\beta]_p,$$

either if $v = s\beta$ and there is an FP rewrite rule $s \to G \mid t$ where $G\beta$ evaluates to *true* or if v is a built-in function call that evaluates to t and β is the empty substitution.

An *FP computation* is a sequence of reduction steps starting from a function call. ∎

As for TRS, the semantics of FP can be based on equational logic.

Def. 11.1.3 (FP Declarative Semantics) An FP rule $s \to G \mid t$ is interpreted as axiom formula $\forall G \to (s = t)$, where $=$ is an equality relation over terms that comes with an equational theory including the built-in functions. ∎

11.2 Embedding FP in CHR

The FP embedding is based on the one for TRS. However, there is no need to flatten the left-hand side of an FP rewrite rule when equations with data terms on the right-hand side are replaced by syntactic equality.

Def. 11.2.1 (Rule Scheme for FP) We translate an FP rewrite rule

$$f(\bar{t}) \to G \mid T$$

into the CHR simplification rule

$$X \text{ eq } f(\bar{t}) \Leftrightarrow G \mid \downarrow(X \text{ eq } T)$$

where X is a new variable and $\downarrow$ is the flattening function.

To the CHR program resulting from the embedding, we also add two helper rules at the beginning of the program for treating data and for mapping built-in functions to built-in constraints.

```
datum   @ X eq T ⇔ datum(T) | X=T.
builtin @ X eq T ⇔ builtin(T) | call(T,X).
```

The **datum** rule syntactically equates and binds the left-hand side variable of an equation to the right-hand side if it is a data term. In the **builtin** rule, the built-in **call(T,X)** calls the built-in constraint that corresponds to built-in function **T** and returns its result in **X**. ∎

Examples FP in CHR

Using partial evaluation, we can apply the two helper rules for data and built-ins already at compile-time to the bodies of the translated CHR rules. We assume so in the following examples for translating FP into CHR.

Example 11.2.1 (TRS Addition in FP and CHR) As in TRS, the FP program for addition of natural numbers is defined by the following two rules, where 0 and **s/1** are data now:

```
0+Y --> Y.
s(X)+Y --> s(X+Y).
```

The embedding of FP rewrite rules into CHR gives:

```
T eq 0+Y <=> T eq Y.
T eq s(X)+Y <=> T = s(T4), T4 eq T5+T6, T5 eq X, T6 eq Y.
```

In contrast to the TRS embedding, the data terms have not been flattened in the heads of the rules. In the body of the second rule, the equation `T eq s(T4)` has been replaced by the syntactic built-in equality `T = s(T4)` by partial evaluation with the **datum** helper rule.

Example 11.2.2 (TRS Conjunction in FP and CHR) The FP program for propositional logic conjunction, where 0 and 1 are data,

```
and(0,Y) --> 0.
and(1,Y) --> Y.
```

results in the following rules in CHR:

```
T eq and(0,Y) <=> T = 0.
T eq and(1,Y) <=> T eq Y.
```

where the body of the first rule is simplified into a built-in equality by partial evaluation.

Example 11.2.3 (Fibonacci Numbers in FP and CHR) We give a recursive FP function for computing Fibonacci numbers (cf. Example 6.2.1), where numbers are data, and the arithmetic operations +/2 and -/2 are built-ins here.

```
fib(0) --> 1.
fib(1) --> 1.
fib(N) --> N>1 | fib(N-1)+fib(N-2).
```

This FP program results in the CHR rules:

```
T eq fib(0) <=> T=1.
T eq fib(1) <=> T=1.
T eq fib(N) <=> N>1 |
     call(N-1,N1), F1 eq fib(N1),
     call(N-2,N2), F2 eq fib(N2), call(F1+F2,T).
```

11.2.1 Structure Sharing as Functional Dependency for Memoization

For efficiency, we can introduce a helper rule that expresses *structure sharing*. In structure sharing data structures share common parts to save memory and increase efficiency. With structure sharing, changes can be made to an immutability data structure without the need to copy the entire structure.

The helper rule makes use of functional dependency, a concept from database theory. It holds when one or more arguments of a relation uniquely determine the value of another argument of the relation. The `fd` simpagation rule has to come first in the program.

```
fd @ T1 eq T \ T2 eq T <=> T1=T2.
```

For deterministic functions, the result of evaluating `T` is unique and therefore determines `T1` and `T2` to be of the same value. This rule in effect propagates syntactic equality of terms upwards in their equation representation and at the same time removes one of the resulting duplicate `eq` equations so that data structures are shared.

We can utilize the `fd` rule to introduce memoization into FP. If a function should be memoized, it suffices to turn all its simplification rules into propagation rules in the CHR embedding.

Example 11.2.4 (FP Fibonacci Numbers with Memoization)
When the function `fib` is declared to be memoized, we get:

```
T eq fib(0) ==> T=1.
T eq fib(1) ==> T=1.
T eq fib(N) ==> N>1 | call(F1+F2,T),
                F1 eq fib(N1), call(N-1,N1),
                F2 eq fib(N2), call(N-2,N2).
```

With the helper rule `fd`, we can memoize, i.e. merge, reuse and remove, identical calls. This results in a linear number of recursive calls as in the CHR version of Fibonacci numbers with memoization.

11.3 Embedding Higher-Order Functions in CHR

A *higher-order function* is a function that passes around functions as arguments. In order to translate a higher-order function into CHR rules, an auxiliary function `apply(F, Args)` is used. This function applies the given function F to the list of arguments `Args`.

Def. 11.3.1 (Higher-Order Function apply) We define `apply/2` by a helper rule in CHR. It uses `const(F)` and `list(Args)` built-ins to check if F is a constant and `Args` is a list.

```
hof @ X eq apply(F,Args) <=> const(F), list(Args) |
    univ(T,[F|Args]),
    X eq T.
```

The built-in `univ(T,L)` holds if L is a list whose head is the function symbol of term T and whose tail consists of the arguments of the term. ∎

With the rule, the query `A eq apply(and,[0,1])` results in `A eq and(0,1)`. We can also apply a function that is a data constructor, a function symbol for data terms. For example, if name is a data constructor, then the query `X eq apply(name,[sue,smith])` yields `X eq name(sue,smith)` and then `X = name(sue,smith)` with the datum rule.

The apply notation can be generalized to allow for the partial application of a function. It fixes the first arguments of a function and produces another function that takes the remaining arguments. The first argument of `apply/2` is now a partial function call instead of a function symbol. The built-in func holds if its argument is function call. The built-in concat concatenates two lists into a third one.

```
hopf @ X eq apply(S,Args) <=> func(S), list(Args) |
    univ(S,SList),
    concat(SList,Args,TList),
    univ(T,TList),
    X eq T.
```

For example, the query `X eq apply(and(1),[0])` yields `X eq and(1,0)`.

Example Higher-Order Functions

Example 11.3.1 (Higher-Order Function `twice`)   The classical example of a higher-order function, `twice`, takes two arguments: a unary function `F`, and a value `A`. It applies the unary function `F` to the value `A` twice.

```
twice(F,A) --> apply(F,[apply(F,[A])])
```

The resulting CHR embedding is the rule:

```
T eq twice(F,A) <=>
    T eq apply(F1,L1),
    F1 eq F,
    L1 eq [X1],
    X1 eq apply(F2,L2),
    F2 eq F,
    L2 eq [A1],
    A1 eq A.
```

The rule after partial evaluation by applying the helper rules for data terms for the lists `L1` and `L2` as well as for structure sharing between `F1` and `F2` becomes:

```
T eq twice(F,A) <=>
    T eq apply(F1,[X1]),
    F1 eq F,
    X1 eq apply(F1,[A1]),
    A1 eq A.
```

For example, assume an increment function `inc` over numbers:

```
inc(X) --> number(X) | X+1.
```

Then the query `X eq twice(inc,6)` leads to `X = 8`.

Higher-order functions are extensively used for list processing in FP.

Example 11.3.2 (Higher-Order Function map) The higher-order function `map` applies a given unary function to each element of a list and returns a list with the results:

```
map(F,[]) --> [].
map(F,[X|Xs]) --> [apply(F,[X])|map(F,Xs)].
```

When the map function is applied to an empty list, it returns an empty list. For non-empty lists, the `map` function applies the unary function `F` to the head of the list, and proceeds recursively with the tail of the list.

For example, the evaluation of the query `X eq map(inc, [1,2,3,4,5])` leads to `X=[2,3,4,5,6]`, because the function `inc` is applied to each element of the list `[1,2,3,4,5]`. ∎

Example 11.3.3 (Higher-Order Function foldr) The higher-order function `foldr` (fold from right) folds a list. *Folding* basically means that the binary function `F` is put between each element of the list.

```
foldr(F,Z,[]) --> Z.
foldr(F,Z,[X1|Xs]) --> apply(F,[X1,foldr(F,Z,Xs)]).
```

The function `foldr` has two rules. When the list is empty the function returns the value `Z`, and when the list is non-empty the function applies the binary function `F` to the head of the list and the result of recursively applying the function `foldr` to the tail of the list.

For example, in the query `X eq foldr(+,0,[1,2,3,4,5,6]))`, the function `foldr` is applied to the list `[1,2,3,4,5,6]` with the binary function `+` and the final value `0`, resulting in `X=21`, the sum of the elements. The query `X eq foldr(*,1,[1,2,3,4,5,6]))` results in `X=720`.

11.4 Embedding Lambda (λ) Abstraction in CHR

In functional programming, λ (lambda) abstraction is a way to create anonymous (unnamed, nameless) functions. The approach is similar

74

to γ (gamma) abstraction in GAMMA. Lambda abstraction allows for functions to be defined and passed around just like any other value. A lambda abstraction consists of a parameter list and a function call. When a lambda abstraction is applied to an expression, every occurrence of the parameter variables in the function call is replaced with the corresponding parameter value taken from the expression.

Computations can be expressed entirely using lambda abstractions, this results in the theory of the lambda calculus, the formal basis of most FP languages. Here we used equational logic to define the declarative semantics of FP to stress the relationship with TRS.

We extend the syntax for the first argument of `apply/2` to allow for such anonymous functions.

Def. 11.4.1 (Function `apply` with λ Abstraction) The `apply/2` function is extended with an additional helper rule to apply an anonymous function `Vars:E` to the given list of arguments `Args`. The notation `Vars:E` denotes a lambda abstraction where `Vars` is the parameter list and `E` is the function call.

```
X eq apply(Vars:E,Args) <=>
  list(Vars), func(E), list(Args) |
    copy(Vars:E,VarsC:EC), Args = VarsC,
    X eq EC.
```

The built-in `copy(A,B)` syntactically equates B with a copy of A. ∎

We make a copy of the lambda abstraction term with new variables, so that variables in the lambda abstraction remain unbound. This allows for the anonymous function to be applied to different arguments without changing the definition of the function.

For example, `X eq [Y]:Y*Y` is an anonymous function for squaring. The query `X eq twice([Y]:Y*Y,7)` yields X=2401, because applying Y*Y to 7 gives 49 and applying Y*Y to it a second time gives 2401. The query `X eq map([Y]:Y*Y,[1,2,3,4,5,6]))` yields X=[1,4,9,16,25,36].

11.5 Embedding CHR Subset in FP

We extend the translation algorithm for CHR simplification rules into TRS from Chapter 10.3 to enable embedding of rules with built-in constraints and guards into FP. Built-in constraints are first rewritten to *eq* equations like CHR constraints. Guards are left unchanged but must not contain output variables from the rule body including the root variable. If this condition does not hold, an embedding into FP is not possible. We also have to classify CHR constraint symbols into two disjoint kinds, function symbols and data constructors. In the rule heads, all constraint symbols must be data constructors except for the constraint symbol that occurs in the equation for the root variable which must be a function symbol. If this classification fails, an embedding into FP is not possible.

Example 11.5.1 (Levenshtein Distance) Recall the CHR program for the edit distance from Exercise 6.4. After replacing `ldist(A,B,C)` by equation `C eq ldist(A,B)` according to our algorithm, the CHR program becomes:

```
LD eq ldist([],Ys) <=> LD eq length(Ys).
LD eq ldist(Xs,[]) <=> LD eq length(Xs).
LD eq ldist([X|Xs],[X|Ys]) <=> LD eq ldist(Xs,Ys).

LD eq ldist([X|Xs],[Y|Ys]) <=> X \= Y |
    LD1 eq ldist([X|Xs],Ys),
    LD2 eq ldist(Xs,[Y|Ys]),
    LD3 eq ldist(Xs,Ys),
    LD eq 1 + min(LD1, min(LD2, LD3)).
```

The translation from CHR to FP finally yields the functional program:

```
ldist([],Ys) --> length(Ys).
ldist(Xs,[]) --> length(Xs).
ldist([X|Xs],[X|Ys]) --> ldist(Xs,Ys).

ldist([X|Xs],[Y|Ys]) --> X \= Y |
  1 +
  min(ldist([X|Xs],Ys),min(ldist(Xs,[Y|Ys]),ldist(Xs,Ys))).
```

11.6 Comparison FP, TRS, GAMMA and CHR

Functional Programming (FP) and Term Rewriting Systems (TRS) are closely related. Both allow for the manipulation and transformation of ground terms by rewriting. Both can be formally based on equational logic, although FP is usually based on lambda calculus.

FP focuses on the definition of functions and their application. TRS is restricted to the symbolic manipulation of terms, which means that all functionality must be defined with rewrite rules. In contrast, FP extends TRS by adding built-in functions and guard conditions as well as a distinction between data terms and function calls. CHR, on the other hand, manipulates multisets of relations called constraints that can contain unbound logical variables. Certain subsets of CHR simplification rules can be embedded in TRS and FP by rewriting relational constraints into equations.

Recall that a GAMMA pair consists of a condition and of functions over molecules. These functions can be defined in FP and then embedded in CHR together with GAMMA. So GAMMA can be seen as a multiset transformation overlay for FP.

11.7 Exercises FP

Exercise 10: Functional Programming

1. Define the bottom-up Fibonacci `fib/3` function with three arguments, two subsequent Fibonacci numbers and a counter. To compute `fib(N)`, one calls `fib(0,1,N)`.

2. Define the function `make_list` that given a positive natural number, returns a list with all numbers from that number down to 1.

3. Define the function `incListBy` that increments the elements of a list by a given number using the higher-order function `map` with a partial function, for example:

   `incListBy(3, [1,2,3])` yields `[4,5,6]`

4. Define the function **append** that concatenates two lists, for example:

```
append([1,2,3], [4,5,6]) yields [1,2,3,4,5,6]
append([], [1,2,3]) yields [1,2,3]
```

5. Define the function **appendall** that concatenates the lists in a list using **foldr** and **append**, for example:

```
appendall([[1,2], [3,4], [5,6]]) yields [1,2,3,4,5,6]
appendall([[], [], [1]]) yields [1]
```

Exercise 11: Higher-Order Functions

1. Define the higher-order function **zipWith** that goes though two lists of the same length in parallel and applies a binary function to the their elements, for example:

```
zipWith((+), [1,2,3], [2,3,4]) yields [3,5,7]
```

2. Define the function **zip** that pairs elements from two lists with a data constructor comma ',' using **zipWith**, for example:

```
zip([1,2,3], [2,3,4]) yields [(1,2),(2,3),(3,4)]
```

3. Analogously to **foldr**, there is the function **foldl** (fold from left). The two functions make a difference if the function used for folding is not associative. Define the function **foldl** in an analogous way to **foldr**. Give an example where the difference matters.

4. Define the function **reverse** that reverses a list using **foldl**.

Selected Solutions

Functional Programming

```
% 1
fib(_,M,0) --> M.
fib(N,M,I) --> I>0 | fib(M,N+M,I-1).


% 2
make_list(0) --> [].
make_list(N) --> N>0 | [N|make_list(N-1)].


% 3
incListBy(N,Xs) --> map('+'(N),Xs).


% 4
append([],Ys) --> Ys.
append([X|Xs],Ys) --> [X|append(Xs,Ys)].


% 5
appendall(Xss) --> foldr(append,[],Xss).
```

Higher-Order Functions

```
% 1
zipWith(_,[],[]) --> [].
zipWith(F,[X|Xs],[Y|Ys]) -->
    [apply(F,[X,Y])|zipWith(F,Xs,Ys)].


% 2
zip(Xs,Ys) --> zipWith((',',),Xs,Ys).


% 3
foldl(F,Z,[]) --> Z.
foldl(F,Z,[X|Xs]) --> foldl(F,apply(F,[Z,X]),Xs).


% 4
reverse(Xs) --> foldl([Ys,Y]:[Y|Ys],[],Xs).
```

Part III

RULE-BASED SYSTEMS

Rule-based systems are characterized by practical implementations rather than theoretical formal models. They include decision-support systems (expert systems, XPS) and advanced database management systems (DBMS). These systems have rules with features that proved useful in practice, with less emphasis on formal considerations, well-defined semantics and properties like declarativity. We will discuss:

- Production Rules (PR): for decision-support systems where rules operate on facts describing knowledge.

- Event-Condition-Action (ECA) Rules: for active database systems where rules can react to events and as Business Rules for workflow systems to model business processes.

- Logical Algorithms (LA): a formalism for deriving and deleting data using logical inference rules, intended for the analysis of programs. LA is related to PR and therefore presented in this part.

- Datalog: a deductive database language for querying and deriving data using logical inference rules. DL is related to LA and PR.

These rule-based systems transform data in the form of knowledge-base facts (PR), database tuples (ECA) or logical atoms (LA, DL).

Production rule systems were the first rule-based systems to be developed. They were created in the 1970s. Production rules (PR) operate by matching facts stored in a knowledge base that satisfy a given condition and then by executing an action. *Event-Condition-Action (ECA)* rules are an extension of PR for active database systems. ECA rules are triggered by events such as updates to the database or external stimuli and respond by executing a corresponding action. ECA rules had their peak in the 1990s, and some aspects of them like recursion have been introduced in the database query language SQL-3 [25] in 1999.

Business rules are a more recent commercial approach to rule-based systems, first appearing in the late 1990s. They are essentially ECA rules but are employed over the whole workflow of a company to automate business processes and to support decision making. They specify and enforce the business logic of a company. They govern activities such as financial transactions, customer interactions, and internal operations. They can enforce compliance with company policies, industry regulations, and legal requirements.

Logical Algorithms (LA) can be considered a declarative production rule language based on logical inference rules. LA was introduced as a formalism for program analysis in the early 2000s. Closely related to LA is *Datalog (DL)* for deductive databases, which was already introduced in the late 1970s as a subset of the logic programming language Prolog.

Chapter 12

Production Rules (PR)

We start with a short history of production rule systems. In the 1970s, MYCIN was a first expert system, written in the Lisp programming language, for diagnosing and treating infectious diseases, developed at Stanford University. OPS5 (Official Production System, version 5) [16] was an influential rule-based language and decision support system developed in the late 1970s at Carnegie Mellon University. It was initially written in Lisp and was used to develop an expert system called R1/XCON for configuring VAX computers.

In the mid 1980s, CLIPS [47], initially written in C, was developed at NASA. It was designed to be a tool for building expert systems and is now available open-source. In the mid 1990s, an extension of CLIPS called JESS [26] was a Java-based rule engine developed at Sandia National Labs. It is now available closed-source but not maintained anymore. Around the same time, the term business rule management system was coined.

In the early 2000s, Drools was written in Java and was integrated into the JBOSS enterprise application platform by firm Red Hat. In the mid 2000s, IBM developed an expert system shell named Watson (written in Java, C++ and Prolog). In the late 2000s, IBM integrated JRules (developed since the mid 1990s by ILOG) into its IBM WebSphere software product line as IBM Operational Decision Manager. Today, all major software companies offer business rule management systems.

12.1 PR Syntax and Semantics

Production rules (PR) are used to infer new information or take actions based on a current state of the system. The rules manipulate facts from a knowledge base which are present in the *working memory*. *Facts* have a name and named attributes similar to records or objects. Each production rule (if-then rule) consists of an if-clause and a then-clause. The *if-clause (condition)* consists of expression matchings describing facts. *Expression matchings* for facts are *patterns* that involve in-place conditions on attributes. The *then-clause* contains actions. *Actions* include the explicit insertion, deletion and updates of facts, performing IO statements, and calling auxiliary functions. In the following, we use OPS5 as a prototypical approach for PR.

Def. 12.1.1 (PR Syntax) A production rule in OPS5 is of the form

(p N LHS --> RHS)

where p indicates a production rule, N is the name of the rule, LHS is the left-hand side (if-clause) and RHS is the right-hand side (then-clause) of the rule.

The LHS consists of *patterns* for facts of the form

{(FN ^AN <V> Cond ...) <ID>}

where FN is the name of the fact, AN is the name of an attribute, V is a variable for the value of the attribute, Cond is an optional condition on the value of the attribute, ID is an optional identifier for the matched fact to be used in the RHS of the rule. *Negated patterns* are preceded by a minus sign -.

In the RHS, facts are introduced, updated and removed using the forms

(make FN ^AN (compute Expr) ...)
(modify <ID> ^AN (compute Expr) ...)
(remove <ID> ^AN (compute Expr) ...)

where Expr is an expression to compute the new value of an attribute.
∎

Production rule systems use a conflict resolution strategy to determine which rule to execute next. During an execution step, all production rules are identified which are applicable. One of the applicable rules is selected using conflict resolution and the then-clause of the selected rule is executed.

Def. 12.1.2 (PR Semantics) A PR *recognize-act cycle* consists of the following steps:

- **Find** all rules with an if-clause whose positive patterns are satisfied by matching facts in the working memory while there are no facts satisfying negated patterns.

- **Select** rule from the set of applicable rules with the help of a *conflict resolution strategy.*

- **Apply** the selected rule by executing its then-clause.

The recognize-act cycle is repeated until no more rule is applicable. ∎

12.2 Embedding PR in CHR

For embedding PR in CHR, facts can be translated to CHR constraints where attribute names are mapped to argument positions. Production rules can be translated to CHR PGR simpagation rules, where the if-clause, with pattern and condition separated, forms head and guard, and where the then-clause forms the body of the CHR rule. Creation, insertion and deletion of facts is implicit in CHR by putting them in the appropriate positions in the head or body of a simpagation rule.

Def. 12.2.1 (Rule Scheme for OPS5 PR) An *OPS5 production rule*

```
(p N LHS --> RHS)
```

is translated into a CHR PGR generalized simpagation rule

```
N @ LHS1 \ LHS2 ⇔ LHS3 | RHS'.
```

Facts (FN ^AN <V> ...) are replaced by CHR constraints FN(V,...),
where attribute names in facts are mapped to argument positions in
the constraint.

The LHS of the production rule is divided into three parts: LHS1,
LHS2, and LHS3. LHS1 represents the patterns of LHS for facts that
are not modified in the RHS, while LHS2 represents the patterns of LHS
for facts that are modified in the RHS. LHS3 represents the conditions
occurring the LHS. The RHS of the production rule is modified such
that the explicit deletion of facts is removed, facts are represented as
CHR constraints and other expressions as built-ins, resulting in RHS'.

Queries consist of the translated facts from the working memory.

■

Examples PR in CHR

We illustrate the embedding with some examples from the OPS5 literature.

Example 12.2.1 (PR Fibonacci Numbers) We start with a production rule to compute Fibonacci numbers bottom-up.

```
(p next-fib
   (limit ^is <limit>)
   {(fibonacci ^index {<i> <= <limit>}
                ^this-value <v1>
                ^last-value <v2>) <fib>}
   -->
   (modify <fib> ^index (compute <i> + 1)
                ^this-value (compute <v1> + <v2>)
                ^last-value <v1>)
   (write (crlf) Fib <i> is <v1>)
)
```

The rule is named **next-fib**. The if-clause expects the fact named
limit in the working memory whose attribute **is** specifies the highest Fibonacci number to be computed, and there must be a fact
fibonacci that represents two subsequent Fibonacci numbers. In
the then-clause, the matched fact will be modified by updating its

index to `<i>+1`, its current value to `<v1>+<v2>` and its last value to `<v1>`. Also, it writes a newline character and the current Fibonacci number on the output.

The above production rule is translated into CHR.

```
next_fib @ limit(L), fibonacci(I,V1,V2) <=> I=<L |
            fibonacci(I+1,V1+V2,V1), nl, write(fib I = V1).
```

The rule head is composed of the CHR constraints `limit(L)` and `fibonacci(I,V1,V2)` which correspond to the facts and their attributes in the if-clause of the production rule. The body is composed of the CHR constraints `fibonacci(I+1,V1+V2,V1)` for the modified fact and the built-ins `nl, write(fib I = V1)` which correspond to the then-clause of the production rule.

The next example shows how the production rules for the Euclidean algorithm for finding the greatest common divisor (GCD) are translated into CHR rules.

Example 12.2.2 (PR Greatest Common Divisor)   In OPS5, the greatest common divisor (GCD) of two numbers can be computed by these four rules:

```
(p done-no-divisors
        (euclidean-pair ^first <f> ^second 1) -->
        (write GCD is 1) (halt) )

(p found-gcd
        (euclidean-pair ^first <f> ^second <f>) -->
        (write GCD is <f>) (halt) )

(p switch-pair
{(euclidean-pair ^first <f> ^second {<s> > <f>}) <e-pair>} -->
(modify <e-pair> ^first <s> ^second <f>))

(p reduce-pair
{(euclidean-pair ^first <f> ^second {<s> < <f> }) <e-pair>} -->
(modify <e-pair> ^first (compute <f> - <s>)))
```

The rule **done-no-divisors** checks if the second number in the **euclidean-pair** is 1, if it is then it writes **GCD is 1** and halts the program. Similarly, the rule **found-gcd** checks if the first and second numbers of the **euclidean-pair** are equal, and then it writes **GCD is** followed by the first number and halts. The rule **switch-pair** checks if the second number in the **euclidean-pair** is greater than the first number, and then modifies the **euclidean-pair** to switch (swap) the first and second number. The rule **reduce-pair** checks if the second number in the **euclidean-pair** is less than the first number, and then modifies the **euclidean-pair** by subtracting the second number from the first number.

The embedding into CHR results in the simplification rules:

```
done-no-divisors @ euclidean_pair(First,1) <=> write(GCD is 1).

found-gcd @ euclidean_pair(First,First) <=> write(GCD is First).

switch-pair @ euclidean_pair(First,Second) <=> Second>First |
          euclidean_pair(Second,First).

reduce-pair @ euclidean_pair(First,Second) <=> Second<First |
          euclidean_pair((First - Second), Second).
```

12.3 Negation-as-Absence (NAA) in CHR

Negation-as-absence (NAA) is a feature that allows for the handling of negated patterns in rules. These negated patterns specify a condition that should not be satisfied by any fact in the working memory. NAA can result in compact rules, but it has some drawbacks. It can be inefficient, as the rule has to check all the facts in the working memory to ensure that no fact satisfies the negated condition.

This common way to handle negation in rule-based approaches and knowledge representation is based on the *closed-world assumption (CWA)*. Under the CWA, we assume that everything not derived is false as it does not exist. NAA checks for absence of negated facts. Under CWA, the addition of facts can invalidate previous rule applications. This means that NAA may give different results when new information is added. We call this behavior *nonmonotonic*.

On the other hand, classical first-order predicate logic is *monotonic*. This property means that the addition of formulas to a theory allows for the derivation of more logical consequences, but never less. Similarly, in declarative rule-based programming languages such as CHR, the addition of rules to a program or constraints to a state allows for more rule applications, never less.

We will implement negation-as-absence (NAA) not only for PR, but for CHR in general. In this way, NAA can be used for any rule-based approach that is embedded in CHR and we will do so for some of the upcoming ones. Our implementation in CHR uses a source-to-source translation that replaces a CHR rule with NAA by CHR rules without negation. To handle NAA, we make use of the auxiliary CHR constraints **check** to check for the absence of a fact and **naa** to trigger the check. Both constraints require the refined semantics of CHR to ensure that the rules for NAA are tried in the right order to implement the nonmonotonicity of NAA.

Def. 12.3.1 (Rule Scheme for CHR with Negation (NAA))

A CHR generalized simpagation rule with a unique identifier **Id** and negated patterns -(NH1, NC1) to -(NHn, NCn), where the **NHi** consist of CHR constraints and negated patterns and where the **NCi** are built-in constraints, and where variables in a negated pattern either occur in head, guard or only in one pattern,

```
Id @ H1 \ H2 ∧ -(NH1,NC1) ... -(NHn,NCn) ⇔ C | B
```

translates to the following CHR rules without negation:

```
probe-Id @ naa ∧ H1 ∧ H2 ⇒ C | check(Id,Vars)
check1-Id @ NH1 \ check(Id,Vars) ⇔ NC1 | true
...
checkn-Id @ NHn \ check(Id,Vars) ⇔ NCn | true
apply-Id @ H1 \ H2 ∧ check(Id,Vars) ⇔ B
```

where there is one **checki-N** rule for each negated pattern -(NHi,NCi) and where **Vars** is the list of the variables in the head H1, H2 and the guard C.

In queries, we add the constraint **naa** at the end. ∎

The first rule **probe-Id** is a propagation rule that fires in a given state when the phase constraint **naa** and the positive head parts of the rule with identifier `Id` are present and the guard `C` holds. Phase constraints trigger rule application attempts by occurring in the head of rules. They rely on left-to-right evaluation order of queries under the refined CHR semantics. On firing, the `probe-Id` rule adds a check constraint for the negated part of the rule.

With the following rules `checki-Id` this constraint checks for the absence of the negated facts. If one is present, the check constraint is removed. This makes sure that the last rule cannot apply anymore. So in that case, in effect the given state remains unchanged. Otherwise, the check constraint with the last rule `apply-Id` checks for the presence of the positive parts of the rule head, and if they are still present, it applies the original rule's body and removes the `H2` constraints and itself. The translation relies on the order of the rules, with `checki-Id` rules being tried before `apply-Id`. This order is guaranteed under the refined semantics of CHR.

When a negated pattern occurs inside a negated pattern, we speak of *nested negation*. When we apply the rule scheme, the inner negation will occur in the head of a `checki-Id` rule. In that case we continue to apply the translation rule scheme to the rules with negation until all negations are transformed away.

Examples OPS5 PR with NAA in CHR

The following examples demonstrate how negation-as-absence (NAA) is implemented in CHR. These will be running examples for the upcoming rule-based approaches.

Example 12.3.1 (PR Minimum with NAA in CHR)   The rule `min` uses NAA to find the minimum among a set of numbers. A number is the minimum if there is no other number smaller than it.

```
(p min
        (num ^val <x>)
       -(num ^val < <x>)
        -->
        (make min ^val <x>)
)
```

92

This rule translates to the CHR propagation rule with negation

```
min @ num(X), -(num(Y),Y<X) ==> min(X).
```

and then to CHR rules without negation

```
probe-min @ naa, num(X) ==> check(min,[X]).
check-min @ num(Y) \ check(min,[X]) <=> Y<X | true.
apply-min @ num(X) \ check(min,[X]) <=> min(X).
```

The query num(2), num(1), num(3), naa with the phase constraint naa correctly at the end results in the addition of the fact min(1) as follows. The phase constraint naa fires rule probe-min with num(2) which adds check(min,[2]). The check constraint is removed by rule check-min since together with num(1) it fires the rule where the guard 1<2 holds. Next, the phase constraint naa fires rule probe-min with num(1). Since there is no smaller number, rule check-min does not apply with check(min,[1]). The check constraint fires with rule apply-min and is replaced with min(1). Finally, naa processes num(3) analogous to num(2), so no more change is incurred and the result is num(1).

Example 12.3.2 (PR Transitive Closure with NAA in CHR) The OPS5 production rules compute the transitive closure of a graph represented by a set of directed edges. NAA avoids the generation of duplicate paths and the resulting nontermination.

```
(p init-path
        (edge ^from <x> ^to <y>)
      -(path ^from <x> ^to <y>)
        -->
        (make path ^from <x> ^to <y>)
)

(p extend-path
        (edge ^from <x> ^to <y>)
        (path ^from <y> ^to <z>)
      -(path ^from <x> ^to <z>)
        -->
```

```
        (make path ^from <x> ^to <z>)
)
```

The rule `init-path` initializes the set of paths with the edges of the graph. However, the rule is only applicable if there is no existing path from the same source to the same destination, represented by the negated pattern `-(path ^from <x> ^to <y>)`. This ensures that the rule is only applied once for each edge and prevents the creation of duplicate facts. The rule `extend-path` creates a new path from x to z, if there is an edge from x to y and a path from y to z in the working memory if it is not present yet, preventing the repeated derivation of the same facts. The translation into CHR with and without negation is:

```
% init-path @ e(X,Y), -(p(X,Y),true) ==> p(X,Y).

probe-init-path @ naa, e(X,Y) ==> check(i-p,[X,Y]).
check-init-path @ p(X,Y) \ check(i-p,[X,Y]) <=> true.
apply-init-path @ e(X,Y) \ check(i-p,[X,Y]) <=> p(X,Y).

% extend-path @ e(X,Y), p(Y,Z), -(p(Y,Z),true) ==> p(X,Z).

probe-ext-path @ naa, e(X,Y), p(Y,Z) ==> check(e-p,[X,Y,Z]).
check-ext-path @ p(Y,Z) \ check(e-p,[X,Y,Z]) <=> true.
apply-ext-path @ e(X,Y), p(Y,Z) \ check(e-p,[X,Y,Z]) <=> p(X,Z).
```

NAA can also be used for *default reasoning* which is another form of nonmonotonic reasoning. One assumes the default unless there is evidence to the contrary. The inferred default knowledge can be retracted in the presence of more specific or conflicting information.

Example 12.3.3 (PR Marital Status with NAA in CHR)   A person is either single or married, where single is to be the default.

```
(p status
        (person ^name <x>)
       -(married ^name <x>)
        -->
        (make single ^name <x>)
)
```

The rule states that if a person with a certain name does not have a fact that states that the person is married, then a fact is added stating that the person is single. If a person marries, a fact would be added stating that the person is married, and this would make the rule inapplicable. This means that the fact that the person is single would no longer be added to working memory. Note that the rule does not deal with the retraction of the default `single` if a person becomes married. Such extensions of our running example will be discussed in the next sections. The translation into CHR yields:

```
% status @ person(X), -(married(X),true) ==> single(X).

probe-status @ naa, person(X) ==> check(status,[X]).
check-status @ married(X) \ check(status,[X]) <=> true.
apply-status @ person(X) \ check(status,[X])<=> single(X).
```

The following example encodes *Russell's barber paradox* in CHR. It states that the barber shaves all men that do not shave themselves. The question if the barber shaves himself leads to a paradox. Suppose the barber shaves himself, then he belongs to those whom he does not shave according to the above statement, which contradicts the assumption. Suppose the opposite is true, and the barber does not shave himself, then he himself fulfills the definition of those he shaves, contrary to the assumption. The semantics of the implementation with NAA is however different, the rule neither leads to an inconsistency nor infinite computation which would denote contradiction.

Example 12.3.4 (Barber Paradox with NAA in CHR)   The paradox can be expressed in CHR as follows:

```
% shaves @ man(X), -(shaves(X,X),true) ==> shaves(barber,X).

probe-shaves @ naa, man(X) ==> check(shaves,[X]).
check-shaves @ shaves(X,X) \ check(shaves,[X]) <=> true.
apply-shaves @ man(X) \ check(shaves,[X]) <=> shaves(barber,X).
```

When the query `man(joe)`, `naa` is evaluated, the `probe-shaves` rule adds `check(shaves,[joe])`. The `check-shaves` rule is not applicable since there is no `shaves(joe,joe)`, so then the derived fact

95

`shaves(barber,joe)` is added by the `apply-shaves` rule. The barber shaves Joe.

When the query `man(tim)`, `shaves(tim,tim)`, `naa` is evaluated, the `probe-shaves` rule adds the constraint `check(shaves,[tim])`. The `check-shaves` rule is applicable since there is the fact `shaves(tim,tim)`, and so `check(shaves,[tim])` is removed. No other rule is applicable and the query remains unchanged, Tim shaves himself.

When the query `man(barber)`, `naa` is evaluated, it behaves like the query `man(joe)`, `naa`. So the barber shaves himself. Posing the answer `man(barber)`, `shaves(barber,barber)`, `naa` as a new query then leads to application of the `check-shaves` rule. No new fact is added, the barber still shaves himself. So with NAA there is no paradox.

12.4 Conflict Resolution (CR) in CHR

Conflict resolution (CR) is a technique to determine which rule to apply when several rules are applicable. There are several different strategies to resolve such conflicts, including systematic search techniques, random rule selection and rule priorities. Conflict resolution is nonmonotonic because adding new facts may cause another rule to be selected for application.

The following rule translation scheme allows for incremental conflict resolution for arbitrary CHR rules. Following the *recognize-act cycle*, a **find** rule identifies applicable rules (recognize), conflict resolution selects a rule, and an **apply** rule executes the selected rule (act). The implementation is incremental because it keeps applicable rules between cycles. The conflict resolution strategy is specified in each rule to allow for rule-specific parameters such as priorities.

Def. 12.4.1 (Rule Scheme for CHR Conflict Resolution) A CHR generalized simpagation rule with a unique identifier `Id` and a strategy parameter `P` for the conflict resolution strategy

`Id @ H1 \ H2 ⇔ C | B : P`

translates to two CHR rules

```
find-Id @ H1 ∧ H2 ⇒ C | conflictset([rule(P,Id,Vars)])
apply-Id @ H1 \ H2 ∧ apply(rule(P,Id,Vars)) ⇔ B,
```

where `Vars` is the list of the variables in the head `H1`, `H2` and the guard `C`. ∎

The `find-Id` rule finds applicable rules. If there are constraints matching the head `H1` and `H2` and if the guard holds, the rule adds the applicable rule instance to the conflict set. The `conflictset` constraint contains a list of applicable rules, each represented by its strategy `P`, its identifier `Id` and its variables `Vars`. The `apply-Id` rule is used to apply the selected rule. If the rule head is still present, the rule's body is executed. In a program, we allow for rules without strategy parameter. These rules are left unchanged and will be applied in the usual way.

Additional helper rules collect applicable rules and select one of them according to the conflict resolution strategy.

Def. 12.4.2 (Helper Rules for CHR Conflict Resolution)
The following helper rules are added at the end of the program in the given order:

```
collect @ conflictset([R]) ∧ conflictset(L) ⇔
    conflictset([R|L])
select  @ fire ∧ conflictset(L) ⇔ L=[_|_] |
    select(L,R,L1) ∧ conflictset(L1) ∧ apply(R) ∧ fire
cleanup @ apply(_) ⇔ true
```

In queries, we add the `fire` phase constraint at the end. ∎

The rule `collect` collects applicable rules into one `conflictset` list. Note that new rules are added at the front of the rule list. When the `fire` phase constraint is present, the `select` rule selects the rule to be applied among the applicable rules in the nonempty conflict set. The order of the constraints in the rule body is important. First the constraint `select` selects the rule to be applied and removes it from the conflict set. Next the updated `conflictset` constraint is added. Then the `apply` constraint triggers rule `apply` for the selected rule `R`. Finally, the phase constraint `fire` is called again for another round of conflict resolution. The process ends if the conflictset becomes empty. When the constraints necessary for the rule application have been removed by another rule in the meantime, the `apply` constraint remains and is garbage collected by the `cleanup` rule.

12.4.1 Conflict Resolution Strategies

The parameter P determines the strategy for selecting a rule from the conflict set. The four choices for P discussed are: `dfs`, `bfs`, `random`, and, if P evaluates to a number, it is interpreted as a rule priority.

- The `dfs` search strategy ensures that the rules are applied in a depth-first manner. This means that the constraints just added are the first ones to become active. This strategy is fast but can be unfair or even lead to nontermination, as some rules may be applied more often than others.

- The `bfs` search strategy ensures that the tuples are applied in a breadth-first manner. This means that constraints become active in the order in which they have been added. This strategy is fair, as all rules are applied in a round-robin fashion. It has the disadvantage to create large conflict sets.

- The `random` selection strategy selects a rule randomly. This strategy is fast and fair, as all rules have an equal chance of being selected and the conflict set stays rather small.

- If P evaluates to a number, then the strategy interprets it as a priority value (weight) for the rule. The rule with the highest priority (preference, salience) is selected. The weight can be known at compile-time (static) or computed at runtime (dynamic) based on some properties of the applicable rule. This allows for more control, but is less efficient and less fair than `random` selection.

It is assumed that all given rules have the same strategy.

Def. 12.4.3 (Conflict Resolution Strategy) These helper rules implement the conflict resolution strategies. The auxiliary constraints in the bodies of the rule are built-ins.

```
dfs @ select(L,R,L1) ⇔ L=[rule(dfs,_,_)|_] |
      L=[R|L1].                  % select first newest rule

bfs @ select(L,R,L1) ⇔ L=[rule(bfs,_,_)|_] |
      append(L1,[R],L).          % select last oldest rule

random @ select(L,R,L1) ⇔ L=[rule(random,_,_)|_] |
      random_select(R,L,L1).   % select rule at random

priority @ select(L,R,L1) ⇔ L=[rule(N,_,_)|_],number(N) |
      sort(L,[R|L1]).   % select rule with highest priority
■
```

The rule **dfs** selects the first newest rule from the conflict set. The rule **bfs** selects the last oldest rule from the conflict set. The built-in **append** holds if the concatenation of the first and second list equals the third list. Here it is used to remove the last rule R from the list L, resulting in the list L1. For the **bfs** and **dfs** search strategies to work, the **collect** rule has to add new applicable rules to the front of the list. The built-in **random** selects an element from a list at random. The rule **priority** sorts the conflict set based on the priority value and selects the rule with the highest priority. The built-in **sort/2** sorts a list of elements in ascending order. In the implementation, a smaller number means higher priority. Note that we choose a simple encoding of rule selection for didactic reasons. In actual implementations for priorities, for example a Fibonacci heap is used as a priority queue [53].

Examples Conflict Resolution (CR) in CHR

We consider three examples using three different conflict resolution strategies. We give the translation according to the rule scheme, but do not list the helper rules which are always the same.

Example 12.4.1 (Coin Flip with Random Selection)   The CHR rules for tossing a coin from Example 4.4.1 now use the strategy **random**. Both rules are applicable and it is left to chance to decide which rule should be applied.

```
h @ coin <=> head : random.
t @ coin <=> tail : random.
```

In the translation for conflict resolution, each rule is split into two rules: `find-h` and `apply-h` for head, and `find-t` and `apply-t` for tail.

```
find-h @ coin ==> true | conflictset([rule(random,h,[])]).
apply-h @ coin, apply(rule(random,h,[])) <=> head.

find-t @ coin ==> true | conflictset([rule(random,t,[])]).
apply-t @ coin, apply(rule(random,t,[])) <=> tail.
```

The query `coin, fire` leads to the creation of a conflict set containing both `head` and `tail` rules. The select rule then randomly selects one of the rules, and the corresponding `apply` rule is executed, resulting either in head or tail with equal probabilities.

Example 12.4.2 (Fair Counting with Breadth-First Search)
The challenge is to write a program for a counter that continuously increments a number such that an arbitrary number of such counters are executed in a fair way, i.e. no counter is ignored, all counters eventually proceed. We can achieve this *fairness* with a breadth-first execution of the counter program.

```
% inc @ count(A) <=> nl, write(A), count(A+1) : bfs.

find-inc @ count(A) ==> conflictset([rule(bfs,inc,[A])]).
apply-inc @ count(A), apply(rule(bfs,inc,[A])) <=>
                        nl, write(A), count(A+1).
```

Here is a sample query and its output. We use concrete Prolog runtime system syntax for query (starting with ?-) and resulting answer from now on.

```
?- count(0), count(1000000), fire.
0
1000000
1
```

```
1000001
2
1000002
...
```

When the phase constraint `fire` becomes active, it adds the `inc` rule for both `count` constraints to the conflict set with the help of rule `find-inc`. Conflict resolution with breadth-first execution will choose the earliest rule in the conflict set. It can be found at the end of the list. So the rule `apply-inc` fires with the `inc` rule for `count(0)` and writes 0 and adds `count(1)` which will in turn add a `inc` rule for it to the conflict set, in front of the list. Now conflict resolution chooses `count(1000000)` and so on.

Dijkstra's algorithm efficiently finds the shortest path from a given source node to every other node in a graph where the directed edges have non-negative weights. For example, it can be used for finding shortest routes in a road network when the weights are distances.

Example 12.4.3 (Dijkstra's Shortest Paths with Priority)
Two rules with dynamic priorities can elegantly implement Dijkstra's shortest path algorithm. The CHR rules are defined in terms of the constraints `dist(X,N)` (Node X is in distance N from the starting node) and `edge(X,Y,M)` (there is an edge from X to Y with distance M).

```
d0 @ dist(X,N) \ dist(X,M) <=> N=<M | true.
dn @ dist(X,N), edge(X,Y,M) ==> N1 is N+M, dist(Y,N1) : N.
```

The rule `d0` states that if there is a constraint `dist(X,N)` and another constraint `dist(X,M)` such that N is less than or equal to M, then the constraint `dist(X,M)` with the larger distance is removed. The rule `dn` states that if there is a constraint `dist(X,N)` and an `edge(X,Y,M)`, then the distance from the starting node to the new node Y is the sum of the distance to X and the distance of the edge between X and Y.

Rule `d0` has no priority, so it is immediately applied if it is applicable. Priorities are non-negative numbers. The lower the value, the higher the priority. The elegance of the program lies in using the current distance N as the dynamic priority to apply instances of rule dn first that deal with shorter distances. In this way the program will always choose to extend the path with the shortest distance, leading to an efficient algorithm.

The translation for conflict resolution is:

```
d0 @ dist(X,N) \ dist(X,M) <=> N=<M | true.

find-dn @ dist(A,B), edge(A,C,D) ==>
                   conflictset([rule(B,dn,[A,B,C,D])]).
apply-dn @ dist(A,B), edge(A,C,D) \
           apply(rule(B,dn,[A,B,C,D])) <=>
                   F is B+D, dist(C, F).
```

A query for the algorithm introduces the edges, a starting node S as constraint dist(S,0) and finally the phase constraint fire to trigger CR. For example, consider the following graph:

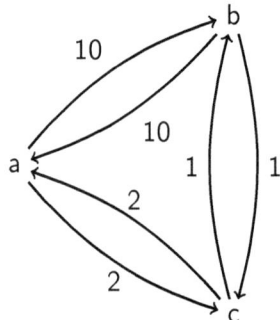

The query

```
?- edge(a,b,10), edge(a,c,2), edge(b,c,1),
   edge(b,a,10), edge(c,a,2), edge(c,b,1),
   dist(a,0), fire.
```

adds the shortest distances dist(b,3), dist(c,2).

12.5 Negation-As-Absence with Conflict Resolution in CHR

So far, we have given separate rule schemes for negation-as-absence (NAA) and conflict resolution (CR). We now integrate both transformations into a single rule scheme. A rule with negation is first translated according to the rule scheme for NAA. The strategy parameter is only kept for the resulting `probe-Id` rule. This rule is then translated according to the rule scheme for CR. The resulting translation can be simplified by using `apply/3` from CR for the NAA check with constraint `check/2`, and by dropping the phase constraint `naa`.

Def. 12.5.1 (Rule Scheme for CHR with NAA and CR) A CHR generalized simpagation rule with a unique identifier `Id`, a strategy parameter `P`, and negated patterns `-(NH1, NC1)` to `-(NHn, NCn)`,

```
Id @ H1 \ H2 -(NH1,NC1) ... -(NHn,NCn) ⇔ C | B : P
```

translates to the following CHR rules:

```
find-probe-Id @ H1 ∧ H2 ⇒ C |
                        conflictset([rule(P,Id,Vars)])
check1-Id @ NH1 \ apply(rule(P,Id,Vars)) ⇔ NC1 | true
...
checkn-Id @ NHn \ apply(rule(P,Id,Vars)) ⇔ NCn | true
apply-Id @ H1 \ H2 ∧ apply(rule(P,Id,Vars)) ⇔ B
```

where `Vars` is the list of the variables in the head `H1`, `H2` and the guard `C`.

In queries, we add the phase constraints `fire` at the end. ∎

12.6 Embedding CHR Subset in PR

In the embedding, CHR constraints become PR facts where argument positions become attribute names.

Def. 12.6.1 (Rule Scheme for CHR Subset in PR) A CHR PGR generalized simpagation rule

```
N @ H1 \ H2 ⇔ C | B
```

translates to a production rule in OPS5

```
(p N LHS -(applied ^Id N ^heads H1) -->
    (make applied ^Id N ^heads H1) RHS)
```

where N is the unique name of the rule, LHS consists of patterns for the head constraints H1 and H2 together with the guard C, and RHS consists of explicit deletions with **remove** for the removable head constraints H2 and explicit insertions with **make** for the body constraints B. The facts for **applied** store the propagation history. The negation-as-absence and subsequent insertion ensure that a rule is only applied at most once the head constraints H1. The handling of the **applied** fact can be removed from the rule if H2 is nonempty, because it is only necessary for CHR propagation rules. ∎

12.7 Comparison PR and CHR

CHR is a declarative formalism, while PR tend to be a more imperative approach. CHR is mainly used to solve constraint-based problems while PR are mainly used to automate and formalize business logics and decisions. Another difference is the syntax, in general PR is more verbose than CHR due to named attributes and explicit insertion, deletion and updates of facts.

Negation-as-absence (NAA) and *conflict resolution (CR)* are important features in production rule systems but they are nonmonotonic. Still they can each be transferred to CHR under its refined semantics using simply source-to-source translation. In this CHR embedding, propagation rules compute applicable rules without adding rule bodies. NAA inhibits the rule application if a negated pattern is present, while CR chooses one rule from the applicable rules for application based on a given strategy. In the other direction, CHR PGR rules are expressible in PR.

12.8 Exercises PR

Exercise 12: Fair Dining Philosophers

Experiment with at least two conflict resolution strategies that solve the dining philosophers problem from Example 9.4 by making the computation fair.

Exercise 13: Dynamic Priorities

Implement a conflict resolution strategy that calculates a priority for a rule according to the function:

$$\text{metricShrink}\,(H_1 \ \backslash \ H_2 \ \Leftrightarrow \ C \mid B) = |B| - |H_2|$$

By this metric rules that remove rather than add constraints are preferred. For example,

```
prime(M) \ prime(N) <=> 0 is N mod M | true :: -1.
```

Use the woodcutter example from Exercise 6.4 to test your implementation.

Chapter 13

Event-Condition-Action (ECA) Rules

Active databases [76] are a type of database management system (DBMS) that include features for automatically responding to certain events or conditions. *Event-Condition-Action (ECA)* rules [14] are an extension of production rules (PR) to provide that kind of event handling. ECA rules are triggered by external or internal events such as updates to the database and respond by executing the corresponding action. The use of ECA rules allows for a more reactive decision-making process, where rules can respond to real-time changes in the state of the system. They can also implement security features, such as auditing and access control. Active databases are used for applications such as event-driven control systems and business process management where ECA rules are known under the name of business rules.

13.1 ECA Rules Syntax and Semantics

A *database relation* is a set of *tuples* (records) where each component of the tuple can be accessed by a named attribute. An ECA *attribute* is a name paired with a data type for its values. Values are often restricted to constants, here we assume they are arbitrary terms and we do not deal with types. Tuples correspond to facts in PR.

Def. 13.1.1 (ECA Rule Syntax and Semantics) ECA rules follow the scheme:

on *Event* **if** *Condition* **then** *Action.*

The *Event* triggers the rule, and the *Action* is the response to the *Event* that occurs when the *Condition* is met.

Events can be internal or external. Internal events are caused by database manipulation and retrieval, and by committing and aborting database transactions (sequences of actions). External events can be temporal (caused by a timer) or stem from other applications. Events can be composed. The most common way is to use Boolean operators. Another way to compose events is to use temporal relationships for events such as time intervals or sequences of events.

Conditions are Boolean expressions. In positive and negated patterns, they have to be able to access database tuples as they are before and as they are after some database manipulation (e.g., old and new attribute values).

Actions include database operations, commitment or rollback of transactions, call of external applications and absorption of events. When an event is absorbed (removed), the action it causes (e.g., an update) will not be executed.

An *ECA database query* is an action.

The *semantics* of ECA rules uses the recognize-act cycle as for production rules (PR) with conflict resolution (CR) and negation-as-absence (NAA), but extended with event handling. ∎

Various database features like integrity constraints, triggers, and view maintenance can be expressed with Event-Condition-Action (ECA) rules. *Integrity constraints* are conditions that must be met in order for a database to be considered *consistent*. These constraints can be placed on attributes within a relation or between relations. Integrity constraints can be maintained by ECA rules by specifying an event that represents a change to the database and a condition that checks if the change violates the constraint.

Triggers are actions that are immediately executed in response to events. They can be directly expressed with ECA rules. A *view* is a virtual relation that is based on the result of a database query. When the data in the underlying relations is updated, the view must also be updated in order to reflect these changes. Such *view maintenance* can be implemented by ECA rules that automatically update the view whenever changes are made to the underlying data. Some *views* can even be made update-able directly by the user. As a side-effect, the underlying base relations from which the view is derived have to be updated, too. Again, this can be accomplished by ECA rules.

13.2 Embedding ECA Rules in CHR

In the CHR embedding, we model events and database tuples as CHR constraints. Also, the updates of database tuples will represented by event constraints, namely `insert/1`, `delete/1`, and `update/2`. The arguments of these constraints are database tuples or patterns for them. The embedding is similar to that of PR in CHR where names of attributes become positions of arguments, but unlike PR, the updates are now explicit. Hence in ECA rules embedded in CHR, tuples can only occur as kept constraints in the rule head, because otherwise they must occur inside update event constraints.

The following rule scheme defines the CHR rules that correspond to these update operations.

Def. 13.2.1 (Rule Scheme for CHR with Database Updates)
Each n-ary relation r generates CHR rules

```
ins @ insert(R) ⇒ R
del @ delete(P) \ R ⇔ copy(P,R) | true
upd @ update(P,P1) \ R ⇔ copy((P,P1),(R,R1)) ∧ R≠R1 | R1
```

where the tuples R and R1 as well as patterns P and P1 are of the form $r(x_1, \ldots, x_n)$ with all variables x_i distinct.

The built-in `copy(A,B)` syntactically equates B with a copy of A. If B is ground this implies that B matches A. In rule **upd**, the built-in *copy*((P,P1),(R,R1)) it is used in the guard to match the ground tuple R against pattern P and at the same time, the copy of patterns (P,P1) is equated with (R,R1), which in effect transfers variable bindings from R to the newly generated tuple R1 according to the patterns.

The inequality R≠R1 ensures termination of the rule in case it would first remove and then insert the same tuple.

In queries, tuples must be ground and the argument R of `insert` must be a ground tuple, while deletion and updates admit a pattern for a tuple where some of its attributes can be variables. For updates, all variables of pattern P1 must occur in P so that the new tuple R1 is ground at runtime. ■

Note that rules **del** and **upd** update *all* tuples that match the pattern. If a tuple is deleted, it is removed from the database and as a consequence, negation-as-absence holds for the tuple. In the CHR embedding, we can include database tuples in queries or generate the database with auxiliary rules.

In addition to these relation-specific rules, additional helper rules are required to absorb the events at the end of the program. This is necessary to ensure that the system does not continue to respond to events that have been processed.

Def. 13.2.2 (Database Updates Event Absorption) The cleanup rules for database operation event removal are added at the end of the program:

```
ins @ insert(_) ⇔ true.
del @ delete(_) ⇔ true.
upd @ update(_,_) ⇔ true.
```
■

In ECA rules embedded in CHR, the composition of events with Boolean operators can be accomplished as follows. Conjunction of events corresponds to mentioning these events in the rule head. Negation can be expressed using negation-as-absence (NAA) from PR. Disjunction of events can be expressed by introducing a copy of the given rule for each event forming the disjunct. Temporal relationships for events can be expressed by adding time stamps to the event constraints as arguments and by imposing built-in constraints on the time stamps.

Example SQL in CHR

In our examples, we do not explicitly deal with conflict resolution to emphasize the main features of ECA rules.

Example 13.2.1 (Limiting Salary Raise) In this classical example, we want to limit the salary increase of an employee to 10 percent. We first give a corresponding ECA rule in the popular database query language SQL. The rule is triggered when the salary of an employee is updated and the new salary is greater than 1.1 times the previous salary.

```
DEFINE RULE LimitSalaryRaise
   IF employee.salary > 1.1 * PREVIOUS employee.salary
   THEN update employee.salary = 1.1 * PREVIOUS employee.salary
```

The keyword `PREVIOUS` refers to the value of an attribute before the current update.

In the CHR embedding, we assume the employee relation `emp/2` consists of a name and a salary attribute. We first use the rule scheme for database updates with patterns:

```
ins @ insert(emp(A,B)) ==> emp(A,B).
del @ delete(emp(A,B)) \ emp(C,D) <=>
      copy(emp(A,B),emp(C,D)) | true.
upd @ update(emp(A,B),emp(C,D)) \ emp(E,F) <=>
      copy((emp(A,B),emp(C,D)),(emp(E,F),emp(G,H))),
      emp(E,F)\==emp(G,H) | emp(G,H).
```

Here are some sample queries illustrating the effect of updates with patterns:

```
?- insert(emp(jon,11)), insert(emp(sue,12)).
emp(jon,11), emp(sue,12)  % Two tuples are inserted

?- insert(emp(jon,11)), insert(emp(sue,12)), delete(emp(X,11)).
emp(sue,12)                    % Tuples with salary of 11 deleted

?- insert(emp(jon,11)), insert(emp(sue,12)), delete(emp(X,Y)).
                               % All tuples are deleted

?- insert(emp(jon,11)), insert(emp(sue,12)),
   update(emp(X,Y),emp(X,10)).
emp(jon,10), emp(sue,10)  % All tuples are updated to salary 10
```

The SQL statement is translated into an ECA rule embedded in CHR. We have to add the resulting rule *before* the rule upd:

111

```
limitRaise-before @ update(emp(Name,S1),emp(Name,S2)) <=>
     S2>S1*1.1 | update(emp(Name,S1),emp(Name,S1*1.1)).
```

In the rule body, the **update** constraint is used with two arguments,
the first argument emp(Name,S1) is the current employee tuple *before*
the update, and the second argument emp(Name,S2) is the tuple after
the update. The rule is triggered before the update happens, so the
condition of the rule is that the salary S2 is greater than S1*1.1. The
action of the rule is to replace the update of the employee tuple with
an update where the new salary is limited to S1*1.1.

We now consider a second version of the rule, where the rule is
added *after* the update rule **upd**:

```
limitRaise-after @ update(emp(Name,S1),emp(Name,S2)) <=>
     S2>S1*1.1 | update(emp(Name,S2),emp(Name,S1*1.1)).
```

The condition of the rule is the same, but the first argument of the
update constraint in the rule body has to be the employee tuple *after*
the update. The action of the rule is to update this new employee
tuple with the limited salary. Note the subtle but essential difference
in the first argument of the **update** constraint (before S1, afterwards
S2) in the bodies of the two rules to achieve the same effect.

Here are two sample queries illustrating the effect of either
limitSalaryRaise rule:

```
?- insert(emp(jon,11)), update(emp(jon,11),emp(jon,12)).
emp(jon,12)              % salary update unchanged
```

```
?- insert(emp(jon,11)), update(emp(jon,11),emp(jon,13)).
emp(jon,12.1)           % update limited to raise of 10%
```

Example of PR with Negation in ECA with Deletion

Since insertion, deletion and updates are explicit in ECA, we can react
to them. In this way, we may be able to avoid negation in the form of
negated patterns. In our example, we write the corresponding ECA
rules directly in CHR.

Example 13.2.2 (PR Marital Status in ECA CHR) Consider
our running Example 12.3.3 about maintaining the marital status of
a person. The original OPS5 PR rule stated that if a person is not
married, their marital status should be single. We are interested in a
version without negation. We will need two rules. We insert `single`
and remove it if the person is already married.

```
% original default rule using insertion events
st1 @ insert(person(X)) ==> insert(single(X)).


% already married, insertion event deleted
st2 @ married(X) \ insert(single(X)) <=> true.
```

We also add new rules so that changes in the marital status are prop-
erly handled:

```
% married overrides, single deleted
st3 @ insert(married(X)), single(X) ==> delete(single(X)).

% react to deletion, re-insert single
st4 @ delete(married(X)), person(X) ==> insert(single(X)).
```

Note that the last rule cannot be expressed without explicit deletion
events.

For example, consider the following three queries and their results:

```
?- insert(person(sue)).
person(sue), single(sue)

?- insert(person(sue)), insert(married(sue)).
person(sue), married(sue)

?- insert(person(sue)), insert(married(sue)),
   delete(married(sue)).
person(sue), single(sue)
```

First a person Sue is inserted into the database by rule `st1`, no other
rule applies. In the second query, her marital status is changed to
married, rule `st1` applies, but the insertion event for `married` triggers

rule st3 which removes single. Third, married is deleted, the event causes rule st4 to apply, resulting in her marital status being set back to single.

13.3 Comparison ECA Rules and CHR

ECA (Event-Condition-Action) rules and CHR are both rule-based languages, but they are used for different purposes. ECA rules are typically used to specify how a database should react to events, such as updates to data. CHR rules, on the other hand, specify how a program should rewrite constraints. ECA rules handle updates explicitly, and so does the embedding in CHR. The update events allow for more control of the execution. This is in contrast to general CHR rules, where insertion and deletion of constraints is implicit. Since ECA can be considered as a generalization of PR, the comparison between PR and CHR also applies to ECA rules. For example, ECA rules feature conflict resolution. As for PR, CHR PGR rules are expressible as ECA rules. ECA events are not needed for the embedding.

13.4 Exercises ECA Rules

Exercise 14: ECA Rules Marital Status

Rewrite the marital status example such that it handles the following relations, where Id is a unique identifier for a person:

```
person(Id,FirstName,LastName)
married(Partner_Id_1,Partner_Id_2)
single(Id)
```

Recall that a person cannot be single and married at the same time, and if persons are inserted, it is first assumed that they are single. Also, if a married tuple is inserted, the second partner takes on the last name of the first partner. For example,

```
?- insert(person(1,peter,mueller)),
   insert(person(2,sarah,schmidt)),
```

```
    insert(married(2,1)).
person(1,peter,schmidt),
person(2,sarah,schmidt),
married(2,1).
```

Selected Solutions

ECA Rules Marital Status

```
% add database update event rules for the involved relations

insert(person(I,_,_)) ==> insert(single(I)).
insert(married(I1,I2)), person(I1,_,LN1), person(I2,FN2,LN2) ==>
    delete(single(I1)),
    delete(single(I2)),
    update(person(I2,FN2,LN2),person(I2,FN2,LN1)).
delete(married(I1,I2)), person(I1,_,_), person(I2,_,_) ==>
    insert(single(I1)),
    insert(single(I2)).
married(I,_) \ insert(single(I)) <=> true.
married(_,I) \ insert(single(I)) <=> true.

% and add clean-up rules for events
```

Chapter 14

Logical Algorithms (LA)

The Logical Algorithms (LA) formalism [45, 46] is basically a declarative production rule language. It can be also considered as a *bottom-up logic programming* language with rule priorities and with explicit permanent deletion. LA was designed as formal means for deriving tight complexity results for algorithms described by logical inference rules, as they occur in program analysis. In [53] a direct translation from the LA into CHR with rule priorities is given, and a translation into regular CHR. These are the only known implementations of LA. They achieve the theoretically postulated optimal complexity results.

14.1 LA Syntax and Semantics

In the LA formalism, programs consist of logical inference rules that manipulate ground atoms that can be marked as deleted.

Def. 14.1.1 (LA Syntax) An *atom* is of the form $a(t_1, \ldots, t_n)$, where a is a predicate symbol of arity $n \geq 0$ and $t_1, \ldots, t_n$ are terms. A *positive* atom A_i can be marked as *deleted*, which is written as $del(A_i)$, where $del/1$ is a special predicate that cannot be deleted.

An *LA program* is a set of *LA inference rules* of the form

$$r @ p : A \to C$$

where r is a unique rule name. The left-hand side (LHS) A is a conjunction of atoms and syntactic or arithmetic comparisons whose

117

variables must occur in the atoms of A, the right-hand side (RHS) C is a conjunction of atoms and arithmetic built-ins whose variables must occur also in A (a case of *range restriction*). The *priority* p is an arithmetic expression, whose variables must occur in a single atom of A. This conditions ensures an efficient implementation of finding the smallest rule priority among the applicable rules. If the priority contains variables, it is called *dynamic*, otherwise *static*. ∎

In the transition system for LA, rule applications add ground atoms.

Def. 14.1.2 (LA Semantics) An *LA state* is a set of ground atoms. In a state, an atom can occur either *positively*, *deleted* or both ways. An *LA initial state (query)* is a state.

An LA rule is applicable to a state if the atoms in the LHS of the rule match atoms of the state in such a way that the positive LHS atoms do not occur also deleted in the state, and the comparisons in the LHS hold under this matching. Additionally, the RHS of the rule instance must not be contained in the state. Finally, there must be no other applicable rule with a higher priority. In the LHS matching and the RHS containment test, a *set-based semantics*, i.e. set inclusion among atoms is used. When a rule is applied, it evaluates its arithmetic built-ins and adds the atoms of its RHS to the state. An *LA final state* is a state where no more rule is applicable. ∎

Note that LA states are *sets* of ground atoms. Such a *set-based semantics* means that there cannot be multiple occurrences of the same atom in a state. This is in contrast to the *multiset-based semantics* of CHR, where duplicates of constraints are allowed. In a set-based semantics, different LHS atoms can match the same atom in a state.

Removal of atoms is modeled in LA by marking atoms as deleted. Since deleted atoms are permanent like positive atoms, no re-insertion of deleted atoms is possible. So deletion makes atoms unavailable for future rule applications. Deletion should not be confused with negation. In LA, we cannot ask for absence of an atom, but we can ask if it was introduced as deleted. Note that LA rule applications only add atoms, atoms are never removed in LA.

14.2 Embedding LA in CHR

LA rules are translated into CHR PGR propagation rules.

Def. 14.2.1 (Rule Scheme for LA Rules) An LA rule with priority p

$$r \mathbin{@} p : A \rightarrow C$$

translates to a CHR PGR propagation rules with priority

$$r \mathbin{@} A_1 \Rightarrow A_2 \mid C : p$$

where A_1 are the atoms of A and A_2 are the comparisons from A. In addition, the rule scheme for set-basedness of upcoming Definition 14.3.2 has to be applied to the rule to generate additional rule variants.
∎

Priorities can be implemented by conflict resolution (CR) as in production rule (PR) systems.

14.3 Permanent Deletion and Set-Based Semantics in CHR

For each LA predicate we introduce CHR PGR simpagation rules for *duplicate elimination* to enforce the set-based semantics and for permanent deletion.

Def. 14.3.1 (Rule Scheme for LA Predicates) For each n-ary LA predicate a/n we add the following simpagation rules at the beginning of the CHR program, where $A = a(x_1, \ldots, x_n)$ and the x_i are distinct variables.

```
A \ A ⇔ true              % Set-basedness of positive atom
del(A) \ del(A) ⇔ true    % Set-basedness of deleted atom
del(A) \ A ⇔ true         % Permanent deletion
```
∎

The first two simpagation rules enforce the set-based semantics of LA. They remove duplicates of positive and deleted atoms, respectively.

Permanent explicit deletion is implemented by the last rule where a positive atom A is removed if its deletion del(A) is present. This last rule causes non-confluence and nonmonotonicity.

To enforce set-based semantics, duplicates are removed. This can cause translated LA rules to become inapplicable in CHR. As a remedy, we create new rule variants that are still applicable even if duplicates have been removed. We introduce the rule scheme for set-based semantics for arbitrary rules in CHR.

Def. 14.3.2 (Rule Scheme CHR with Set-based Semantics)
To a CHR generalized simplification rule

$$H \Leftrightarrow G \mid B$$

for each partition of the head H into $(H_0 \wedge H_1 \wedge H_2)$, where H_1 and H_2 are non-empty, we add the rule

$$H' \Leftrightarrow H_1 = H_2 \wedge G \mid B'$$

where H' is H with duplicate constraints removed and B' is B with duplicate constraints removed. When checking for duplicates, we take into account the guard $H_1 = H_2 \wedge G$. Finally, we apply CHR rule simplification (Section 5.1.1) to the rule. ∎

Rule simplification will remove many generated rules as redundant, because the guard $H_1 = H_2$ will usually fail. Otherwise this approach can cause a combinatorial explosion in the number of rules in case all head atoms of a rule can be equated.

Example 14.3.1 (Set-Basedness) The following LA rule (ignoring priorities and rule names) derives a new atom b(X,Y) if constraints matching a(1,Y) and a(X,2) are in the state.

a(1,Y) ∧ a(X,2) → b(X,Y)

The rule is applicable to the single atom a(1,2) because the atom matches both head atoms a(1,Y) and a(X,2). So the atom b(1,2) will be added. However, when the LA rule is translated into the CHR propagation rule

```
a(1,Y), a(X,2) ==> b(X,Y).
```

the rule is not applicable to the single atom `a(1,2)`. Applying the set-basedness rule scheme, the rule written in generalized simplification rule form is:

```
a(1,Y), a(X,2) ==> a(1,Y), a(X,2), b(X,Y).
```

The generation of additional rule variants, equating `a(1,Y)=a(X,2)`, leads to the additional rule:

```
a(1,Y) ==> a(1,Y)=a(X,2) | a(1,Y), b(X,Y).
```

which can be simplified into the propagation rule

```
a(1,2) ==> b(1,2).
```

With this rule variant, the query `a(1,2)` leads to the desired addition of `b(1,2)` in CHR as in LA.

We can also apply the above rule scheme to CHR constraints to introduce set-basedness and permanent explicit deletion in CHR.

LA Examples

Example 14.3.2 (Dijkstra's Shortest Path Algorithm in LA)
An LA implementation of Dijkstra's efficient single-source shortest path algorithm (Example 12.4.3) is

```
d0 @ 0: dist(X,N) ∧ dist(X,M) ∧ N<M → del(dist(X,M))
dn @ N: dist(X,N) ∧ edge(X,Y,M) → dist(Y,N+M)
```

Rule d0 uses explicit permanent deletion of LA. In the rule, the case N=M needs not to be covered because of the set-based semantics that will remove duplicate atoms.

The resulting CHR embedding is

```
% rules for set-basedness and permanent deletion

d0 @ dist(X,N), dist(X,M) <=> N<M | del(dist(X,M)) : 0.
dn @ dist(X,N), edge(X,Y,M) ==> dist(Y,N+M) : N.
```

There are no rule variants produced for set-basedness: For rule d0 if dist(X,N)=dist(X,M), the guard N<M does not hold. For rule dn, the two head constraints do not unify.

The following example illustrates that permanent deletion cannot deal with changes in general.

Example 14.3.3 (ECA Marital Status in LA)   Recall the ECA CHR rules for the marital status.

```
st1 @ insert(person(X)) ==> insert(single(X)).
st2 @ married(X) \ insert(single(X)) <=> true.
st3 @ insert(married(X)), single(X) ==> delete(single(X)).
st4 @ delete(married(X)), person(X) ==> insert(single(X)).
```

We try to write them in LA, where insertion is implicit and deletion is explicit and permanent.

```
st1  @ person(A) → single(A).
st23 @ married(A) ∧ single(A) → del(single(A)).
st4  @ del(married(A)) ∧ person(A) → single(A).
```

The first rule st1 is the original default rule. Rule st23 implements two rules of the ECA version which become identical with implicit insertion. It states that if a person marries, its status single is deleted. However, due to permanent deletion, a married person can never become single again. So rule st4 can never apply, since single cannot be added back.

14.4 Embedding CHR Subset in LA

To enable embedding of CHR PGR rules in LA we add identifiers to atoms that represent CHR constraints so we can distinguish multiple copies of the same constraints. In this way it enables a multiset-based semantics and thus also re-introduction of deleted atoms.

Def. 14.4.1 (CHR Subset in LA) A CHR PGR generalized simpagation rule with only comparisons in the guard G and only arithmetic built-ins D in the body of the form

```
N : H1...Hi \ H_{i+1}...Hn ⇔ G | D ∧ B1 ... Bm
```

translates to the two LA rules

```
N1 : H1[Id1]...Hi[Idi] ∧ H_{i+1}[Id_{i+1}]...Hn[Idn] ∧
     alldiff(Id1...Idi) ∧ G →
         applyOnce(N,Id1...Idi,Vars)

N2 : lastID(Id) ∧ applyOnce(N,Id1...Idi,Vars) →
         del(lastID(Id)) ∧ lastID(Id+m) ∧
         del(H_{i+1}[Id_{i+1}]) ∧ ... ∧ del(Hn[Idn]) ∧
         D ∧ B1[Id+1] ∧ ... ∧ Bm[Id+m]
```

If there are no body atoms in the original rule (m=0), the atoms `del(lastID(Id))` ∧ `lastID(Id+m)` are removed from the translation.

A CHR query consisting of ground CHR constraints

```
B1 ... Bm
```

is translated to an LA initial state

```
lastID(m) ∧ B1[1] ∧ ... ∧ Bm[m]
```

■

The notation `A[Idj]` in the definition stands for an atom `A` with an additional argument `Idj` which is a natural number acting as unique identifier of the atom. In the rule heads, `Id, Id1...Idn` are new different variables for identifiers. The built-in `alldiff` holds if its arguments are different to each other. It ensures that different atoms are matched in the head of the rule. The atom `lastId/1` keeps track of the last identifier used. New identifiers are generated for the atoms of the body in the rule. `Vars` is the list of variables that occur in the head and guard of the original rule.

If there are no removable constraints, the generalized simpagation rule corresponds to a propagation rule. To avoid trivial nontermination, we introduce an intermediate atom `applyOnce` in the first rule of the translation. It basically serves as a propagation history, similar to the one for Production Rules (PR). In this way it is made sure that the rule cannot be applied a second time in LA.

Example 14.4.1 (ECA Marital Status in LA, contd.) The last rule `st4` for the marital status still cannot be implemented directly in LA, but we can do with a variant written in CHR embedded in CHR:

```
st5 @ person(X), divorce(X) \ married(X) <=> single(X).
```

The resulting embedding in LA is:

```
st51 @ person(A,Id1) ∧ divorce(A,Id2) ∧ married(A,Id3) ∧
         alldiff(Id1,Id2,Id3) →
            applyOnce(st5,Id1,Id2,Id3,[A]).

st52 @ lastID(Id) ∧ applyOnce(st5,Id1,Id2,Id3,[A]) →
            del(lastID(Id)) ∧ lastID(Id+1) ∧
            del(married(A,Id3)) ∧ single(A,Id+1).
```

14.5 Comparison LA, PR, ECA Rules and CHR

Unlike PR, ECA and CHR rules, which feature a multiset-based semantics, LA is *set-based*, which means that there are no duplicates of atoms. To avoid infinite applications of the same rule, in LA one only applies a rule if its body has not been introduced before. This check is sufficient, since atoms are never removed in LA and since LA is set-based. In CHR, on the other hand, a propagation rule is only applied once to the same matching constraints. In this way, re-application is avoided while allowing for removal of constraints.

Like PR and ECA, LA allows for the specification of *rule priorities*, which determines the order in which rules are applied. In regular CHR, the order is determined by the order in which they are written in the program text.

In PR, ECA rules and LA, *deletion* of facts, tuples or atoms is explicit, while it is implicit in CHR. In PR and ECA rules, an atom that deleted can be added back again, while in LA, deletion is explicit and permanent. Insertion is explicit in PR and ECA rules, but implicit in CHR and LA.

LA rules can be embedded as PGR propagation rules in CHR using additional CHR rules to implement set-basedness, permanent deletion and rule priorities. We can translate CHR PGR rules into LA rules when we add identifiers to atoms so that duplicates are possible and deleted atoms can be re-introduced. As an example of cross-fertilization, we can now introduce a multiset-based semantics into LA by adding identifiers to LA atoms. This transformation only works for rules that do not have deleted atoms in the head. Also set-basedness of LA can be transferred to PR and ECA rules as well as GAMMA via the rule scheme that was introduced for CHR.

14.6 Exercises LA

Exercise 15: Set-Basedness for CHR Examples

Apply the LA rule scheme for set-basedness to the introductory CHR programs from Chapter 6, which are minimum, greatest common divisor, prime numbers, Fibonacci numbers, and transitive closure.

Selected Solutions

Set-Basedness for CHR Examples

```
% Minimum
% original CHR rule
min(A) \ min(B) <=> A=<B | true.
% as generalized simplification rule
min(A),  min(B) <=> A=<B | min(A).
% rule variant from set-basedness
min(A) <=> min(A)=min(B),A=<B | min(A).
% redundant after rule simplification
min(A) ==> true | true.


% Primes analogous to Minimum

% Greatest Common Divisor
gcd(N) \ gcd(M) <=> 0<N,N<M | gcd(M-N).     % original CHR rule
gcd(N),  gcd(M) <=> 0<N,N<M | gcd(N), gcd(M-N). % generalized
gcd(N) <=> gcd(N)=gcd(M),0<N,N<M | gcd(N), gcd(M-N). % variant
gcd(N) <=> false | gcd(N), gcd(N-N).              % redundant
```

```
% Fibonacci, original rule
fn @ fib(Max), fib(N2,M2) \ fib(N1,M1) <=> Max>N2, N2 is N1+1 |
            fib(N2+1,M1+M2).
```

For Fibonacci, the `fn` rule variant with `fib(N2,M2)=fib(N1,M1)` implies `N1=N2` which contradicts the guard `N2 is N1+1`.

Transitive closure already uses set-basedness and does not have rule variants. So for the introductory CHR example programs, the rule scheme for set-basedness does not introduce any relevant rule variants.

Chapter 15

Datalog (DL)

Datalog (DL) [17] is a language to represent and query knowledge bases and databases. Unless more traditional database languages, it allows for recursion and negation. It uses inference rules to derive new facts from the facts given in the database. The history of *deductive databases (knowledge bases)* can be traced back to the 1970s with the development of the Prolog logic programming language and the relational database model. The idea behind deductive databases is to extend the relational model with inference rules [41]. Various extensions of Datalog have been proposed, recently [12, 18]. *Answer Set Programming (ASP)* can also be seen as extended variation of Datalog and has been embedded in CHR [70]. DL has been applied to problems in data integration, networking, and program analysis.

DL is similar to Logical Algorithms (LA) in that it features bottom-up propagation rules, but unlike LA it does not provide for the deletion of atoms. However, DL features *negation-as-absence* similar to Production Rules (PR). In DL, this kind of nonmonotonic negation is made more sound by restricting its use. The restriction gives rise to priorities among rules.

15.1 DL Syntax and Semantics

Datalog (DL) is a declarative language for reasoning about knowledge in deductive databases. It is used for making logical inferences using rules over database tuples called *facts*, but it does not support database updates. While DL is a syntactic subset of the logic programming language Prolog, it uses bottom-up rather than top-down evaluation.

DL Syntax DL clauses are logical implications like the rules in LA, but the consequent is restricted to a single atom and the implications are written the other way round, with LHS and RHS exchanged. Terms are restricted to a finite set of constants.

Def. 15.1.1 (DL Syntax) A *DL atom* A is of the form $p(t_1, \ldots, t_n)$ where p is a predicate symbol and the t_i are either variables or taken from a finite set of constants. A *DL literal* is either a positive atom A or a negated atom $\neg A$. A *DL clause* is of the form:

$$A \leftarrow B_1 \wedge \ldots \wedge B_n \ (n \geq 0)$$

where the LHS A is an atom and the RHS consists of literals B_i. A clause with $n > 0$ is a DL *rule* and a clause with $n = 0$ a DL *fact*, written just as A. Every variable that appears in the LHS of a clause or in a negated atom must also appear in a positive literal of the RHS of the clause (a case of a range restriction).

A *DL program (database, knowledge base)* is a set of DL clauses. ∎

Note that a fact cannot contain variables due to the range restriction. DL has no built-ins, but there are extensions that have.

Even though the LHS of DL rules consist of a single atom only, we can express rules with more than one atom on the LHS (like in LA), by replacing

$$A_1 \wedge \ldots \wedge A_m \leftarrow B_1 \wedge \ldots \wedge B_n \ (m > 0)$$

by the set of rules

$$A_i \leftarrow B_1 \wedge \ldots \wedge B_n \text{ for each } A_i$$

This transformation is possible due to the range restriction.

DL Semantics DL has a set-based semantics like LA. DL features nonmonotonic negation, which is essentially negation-as-absence (NAA) as used in PR, but without built-ins. However, in order to ensure that NAA in DL can be used for more sound reasoning, negation must be stratified and safe. *Safeness* holds if the negated atom is ground at the time of execution. This is ensured by the range restriction of DL rules. *Stratification* disallows recursion through negation. To ensure this condition and to improve the evaluation of negations, we assign each predicate to some *stratum* as follows.

Def. 15.1.2 (DL Stratification) A DL program is *stratified* if for each rule

$$A \leftarrow B_1 \wedge \ldots \wedge B_n$$

the stratum for A is higher or equal to the stratums of the positive literals in the RHS and strictly higher than the stratums of the negative literals in the RHS. We associate a rule with the stratum of its LHS atom A. ∎

The semantics of DL is similar to that of LA. The DL rules infer new facts from the existing facts in the database using forward chaining. The inferred facts are added to the state, and the process of forward chaining is repeated until no new facts can be inferred. The final state is the set of all facts that are true in the database.

Def. 15.1.3 (DL Semantics) A *DL state* is a set of ground atoms. A *DL initial state* is a state containing the facts of the database.

A DL rule is applicable to a state if the positive literals of the RHS of the rule match atoms in the state and if the negative literals of the RHS do not match any atoms in the state. Additionally, the LHS of the rule instance must not be contained in the state. Finally, there must be no other applicable rule with a lower stratum. In the RHS matching and the LHS containment test, a *set-based semantics* for atoms is used. When a rule is applied, it adds the atoms of its LHS to the state. A *DL final state* is a state where no more rule is applicable. ∎

The conditions on the applicability of rules ensures that atoms for predicates in a lower stratum are exhaustively derived before they occur in a negation.

Range-restricted propagation rules under set-based semantics mean that the set of atoms than can be derived from an initial state is finite when the set of constants is finite, because rule applications only add atoms. Therefore DL is decidable, DL is not Turing-complete.

15.2 Embedding DL in CHR

Similar to the embedding of LA in CHR, we represent DL atoms as CHR constraints, DL rules as propagation rules and enforce a set-based semantics.

Def. 15.2.1 (Rule Scheme Set-Basedness of DL Predicates)
Each n-ary DL predicate p/n generates a CHR simpagation rule

```
A \ A ⇔ true.
```

where $A = p(x_1, \ldots, x_n)$ with x_i being distinct variables. ∎

DL rules are translated into CHR propagation rules. To ensure that the DL stratification is respected in the computation, we add priorities corresponding to the numeric levels of the strata and can then use conflict resolution like in LA and PR.

Def. 15.2.2 (Rule Scheme for DL Clauses) A *DL rule*

$$A \leftarrow B$$

where A is a single user atom, B is a conjunction of literals, and s is its *numeric stratum*, translates to a CHR PGR propagation rule with priority s

$$B \Rightarrow A : s.$$

To the translated rules we add the derived rule variants from the set-based transformation (Definition 14.3.2) from LA.

A *DL fact* becomes part of the query or is generated by auxiliary rules. ∎

130

15.3 Negation-as-Repair (NAR) in CHR

When embedding the negation of DL into CHR we can use negation-as-absence (NAA) from PR. In addition, we introduce here a specialized implementation that makes use of the range restriction and the fact that the LHS of a DL rule is a single atom. The special case called *negation-as-repair (NAR)* assumes that the negation holds and thus adds the atom, and if it does not, the rule's body atom is removed again.

We define and generalize NAR for a subset of CHR PGR propagation rules. A negated DL atom $\neg A$ will be represented by the general negated form $-(A,\texttt{true})$ known from PR. We generalize negated patterns to allow for built-ins.

Def. 15.3.1 (Rule Scheme for CHR with NAR) A CHR PGR propagation rule with stratified negation and *stratum priority* P

```
N @ H, -(NH1,NC1)...-(NHn,NCn) ⇒ C | B : P
```

where the body B is a single CHR constraint, translates to CHR rules without negation

```
repair-N @ NH1 \ B ⇔ NC1 | true : 0 % eagerly repair
...
repair-N @ NHn \ B ⇔ NCn | true : 0 % eagerly repair
apply-N @ H ⇒ C | B : P                % ignore negation
```
■

The rule scheme only works for propagation rules since adding removed constraints back would lead to another application of rule `apply-N` and so cause nontermination.

In comparison to negation-as-absence (NAA) from PR, the NAR rule scheme adds the rule's body atom B directly in the rule `apply-N` instead of an auxiliary check constraint. The presence of the negated pattern is still checked with each rule `repair-N`, but if the negation does not hold, the rule repairs the situation by removing the atom B. The `repair-N` rules must have the highest priority (here 0), so that the repair is executed before the added atom is further evaluated.

The semantic difference to the NAA translation is that the single body atom B may be removed later in the computation, when the negation ceases to hold because an atom introduced. This leads to a kind of incrementality. Also, a repair-N rule may remove an atom B that was produced by another rule than the given rule. Unlike NAA, the two rules for NAR, apply-N and repair-N, are confluent since they do not share head constraints. This leads to a more declarative form of negation. The result of NAR are shorter and more concise, often incremental and concurrent CHR programs that can be easier analyzed.

PR Examples in DL in CHR with Negation by Repair (NAR)

The examples using NAR show that NAA is not always necessary.

Example 15.3.1 (PR Marital Status with NAR) The DL rule corresponds to the original production rule for marital status.

```
single(X) :- person(X), not(married(X)).
```

The DL rule features stratified and safe DL negation. The predicates person and married have stratum 0, the predicate single has stratum 1. The embedding of the DL rule in CHR using NAR is:

```
% add rules for set-basedness, no rule variants

% CHR embedding with negation
% person(X), -(married(X),true) ==> single(X) : 1.

% CHR embedding without negation using NAR rule scheme
repair @ married(X) \ single(X) <=> true : 0.
apply  @ person(X) ==> single(X) : 1.
```

The two rules generated by the NAR rule scheme, **repair** and **apply**, correspond to the rules st23 and st1 for marital status in LA with explicit deletion (Example 14.3.3). But rule st23 is now the result of the translation of NAR, not added by hand as before. The above code snippet omits the duplicate elimination rules for set-basedness of

132

the three predicates. No rule variants for the set-based semantics are generated.

Example 15.3.2 (PR Transitive Closure in DL and CHR)
We give a DL program for computing the transitive closure based on the one introduced for PR.

```
p(X,Y) :- e(X,Y), not(p(X,Y)).
p(X,Z) :- e(X,Y), p(Y,Z), not(p(X,Z)).
```

The rule is not allowed in DL because it creates a recursion through negation. So the negation is not stratified. Still, the rule can be translated into CHR with NAR.

```
% set-basedness rule
        e(X,Y) \ e(X,Y) <=> true : 0.
% set-basedness and repair rule
repair @ p(X,Y) \ p(X,Y) <=> true : 0.

apply  @ e(X,Y) ==> p(X,Y) : 1.
apply  @ e(X,Y), p(Y,Z) ==> p(X,Z) : 1.
```

The translation of the two given rules with negation results in a simpagation rule for duplicate elimination of paths. This rule has been already produced by the set-basedness rules and is therefore redundant. The set-based rule transformation does not introduce any rule variants. The resulting rules are correct even though the DL version is not stratified.

The redundancy of the repair rule reveals that the DL version of the example does not need the negation in the first place, since DL is set-based. In DL, the following variants of the given rules suffice:

```
p(X,Y) :- e(X,Y).
p(X,Z) :- e(X,Y), p(Y,Z).
```

The rules correspond to the CHR version of transitive closure from Chapter 6.

Example 15.3.3 (PR NAA Barber Paradox in DL) The paradox states that a **barber** shaves a man if he does not shave himself.

```
shaves(barber,X) :- man(X), not(shaves(X,X)).
```

The negation is safe but not stratified because the recursion goes through negation. The translation gives:

```
man(X) \ man(X) <=> true : 0.
shaves(X,Y) \ shaves(X,Y) <=> true : 0.
```

```
repair @ shaves(X,X) \ shaves(barber,X) <=> true : 0.
apply  @ man(X) ==> shaves(barber,X) : 1.
```

The set-based rule transformation considers a rule variant for the **repair** rule where the two **shaves/2** constraints in the head were equated

```
repair @ shaves(barber,barber) ==> true : 0.
```

which is obviously redundant.

The code using NAR is incremental in that it can model the change from being shaved by the barber to shaving oneself using the **repair** rule. A change in the other direction is not possible.

15.4 Magic Set Transformation (MST) in CHR

The *Magic Set Transformation (MST)* is a technique for optimizing the evaluation of DL queries. A database query asks for facts that are in the database or can be derived from it. MST is a way to simulate top-down evaluation using the bottom-up evaluation of DL. The method works by rewriting the DL program such that the rules can only fire when their result, the derived fact, is relevant for the query, reducing the number of unnecessary computations. The DL facts will now be represented by rules, too.

MST adds *query patterns* for atoms to DL rules. A query pattern represents a demand for facts that should be derived in order to answer a query. The original magic set method has to avoid to unbound variables in these patterns for atoms, because DL uses a ground representation. In the CHR embedding we can implement MST in a more general way with patterns that contain variables over terms that can be subjected to built-ins. We generalize from DL rules to a subset of CHR PGR propagation rules with built-ins for guards.

In a query pattern q(P), P is a CHR constraint atom that is used as a pattern. It is supposed to match the instances of the constraint, i.e. the pattern variables stand for arbitrary values and will never be bound during computation. In the rule scheme, we allow for propagation rules with empty heads to be able to temporarily represent DL facts in CHR.

Def. 15.4.1 (Rule Scheme for Magic Set Transformation)
The *query pattern subsumption rule* comes first in the program

```
subsume @ q(P1) \ q(P2) ⇔ match(P1,P2) | true,
```

where P1 and P2 are variables.

Each *extended CHR PGR propagation rule*

```
H1...Hn ⇒ G | B
```

where the head can also be empty and the body B is a single CHR constraint, is replaced by the *query-generating rule*

```
q(P) ⇒ G ∧ copy(P,B) | q(H1)...q(Hn)
```

and by the *query-filtered rule*

```
q(P), H1...Hn ⇒ G ∧ match(P,B) | B,
```

where P is a new variable standing for a pattern.

To the translated rules we add the derived rule variants from the set-based transformation (Definition 14.3.2).

In a query, the CHR constraints are turned into query patterns by wrapping them with q/1. ∎

In MST, a query pattern subsumption rule is added as the first rule in the program. In the guard, the built-in match(P1,P2) holds if P2 is an instance of pattern P1. The rule compares two query patterns and only keeps the more general one. With the rule, the number of such query patterns is kept finite for DL, because each argument of the pattern is either a value from a finite set or a variable whose name does not matter.

Furthermore, each original rule is replaced by two rules, the query-generating rule and the query-filtered rule. The *query-generating rule* inverts the original rule and generates new query patterns for constraints that are needed for the applicability of the original given rule. In the guard, the built-in copy(P,B) syntactically equates B with copy of pattern P with new variables, in effect intersecting pattern P and constraint atom B in B. The rule basically says that constraints matching P can potentially derived from H1,... Hn by a rule application. In case of DL facts, we have that n=0 and the empty head conjunction is represented by *true* in the body of the query-generating rule. The resulting propagation rule is redundant and can be simplified away.

In addition, each original rule is specialized into a *query-filtered rule* by including the query pattern corresponding to its derived constraint. This limits the rule's applicability to only those cases where the derived constraint is potentially needed to answer the query.

Example Magic Set Transformation (MST) in CHR

Example 15.4.1 (Transitive Closure with MST) The CHR propagation rules for transitive closure together with a few sample facts for the edge relation

```
e(X,Y) ==> p(X,Y).
e(X,Y), p(Y,Z) ==> p(X,Z).

% DL facts
% e(1,2). e(2,3). e(3,4). e(4,2).
```

are replaced by the rules according to the set-basedness and MST transformations

```
% query subsumption rule
q(P1) \ q(P2) <=> match(P1,P2) | true.

% add set-basedness rules, no rule variants generated

% query-generating rules
q(P) ==> copy(P,p(X,Y)) | q(e(X,Y)).
```

```
q(P) ==> copy(P,p(X,Z)) | q(e(X,Y)), q(p(Y,Z)).

% query-filtered rules
q(P), e(X,Y) ==> match(P,p(X,Y)) | p(X,Y).
q(P), e(X,Y), p(Y,Z) ==> match(P,p(X,Z)) | p(X,Z).

% query-filtered rules for DL facts
q(P) ==> match(P,e(1,2)) | e(1,2).
...
q(P) ==> match(P,e(4,2)) | e(4,2).
```

For each predicate, we add a set-basedness rule. For each given rule, we add a query-generating rule and a query filtered rule. The first query-generating rule states that if a query pattern `q(P)` is present that can be equated with `p(X,Y)`, then a corresponding instance of the query pattern `q(e(X,Y))` is derived. The second rule similarity derives the query patterns `q(e(X,Y))` and `q(p(Y,Z))`. Note that `Y` is a new variable that violates the range restriction of DL but is feasible in CHR. Each given rule and fact introduces a query-filtered rule, where each rule now only fires if needed, i.e. if the query pattern requires it. Each query-filtered rule introduces a query demand pattern `q(P)` in the head and a guard that checks if the fact that will be derived matches the pattern P.

Two sample queries and their results are

```
?- q(p(4,1)).
q(e(_,_)), q(p(_,1)),
e(1,2), e(2,3), e(3,4), e(4,2)

?- q(p(4,3)).
q(e(_,_)), q(p(_,3)),
e(1,2), e(2,3), e(3,4), e(4,2),
p(1,3), p(2,3), p(3,3), p(4,3)
```

The query for `p(4,1)` returns no path. From the query pattern in the answer we can see that there is no path in the database that ends in 1. However, the query for `p(4,3)` returns that path. From the answer we can see that all paths ending in 3 are needed to compute the result.

15.5 Magic Set Transformation with Negation-as-Repair in CHR

Negation-as-Repair (NAR) can be incorporated into MST for CHR rules that correspond to Datalog (DL) rules over arbitrary terms. Basically we apply first MST and then the NAR rule scheme. In MST, a negation with built-ins `-(NH,NC)` leads to a query pattern `q(NH)`. After the MST transformation, the query-filtered rule will contain the negation and be subjected to the NAR transformation.

Def. 15.5.1 (Rule Scheme for CHR with MST and NAR)
A CHR PGR propagation rule with negation and a single CHR constraint B as body

```
N @ H1...Hn, -(NH1,NC1)...-(NHm,NCm) ⇒ C | B : P
```

translates to CHR rules with the DL MST applied and without negation

```
% MST query-generating rule with patterns for negation
N @ q(P) ⇒ C ∧ copy(P,B) | q(NH1)...q(NHm), q(H1)...q(Hn)

% NAR repair rules
repair-N @ NH1 \ B ⇔ NC1 | true
...
repair-N @ NHm \ B ⇔ NCm | true

% MST query-filtered rule from NAR without negation
apply-N @ q(P) ∧ H1...Hn ⇒ C ∧ match(P,B) | B
```
■

The query patterns for the negations come first in the body of the query-generating rule to make sure that relevant facts are derived before the rule in query-filtered form is applied. Then the stratum derived from the use of negation in DL can be dropped, because the query patterns take care of the right rule application order.

Example MST with NAR in CHR

Example 15.5.1 (PR Marital Status with MST and NAR)

The given CHR PGR propagation rule with negation and DL facts

```
person(X), -(married(X),true) ==> single(X).
```

```
% DL facts
% person(sue). person(sam). married(sam). married(fred).
```

are replaced by the query subsumption rule, the set-based rules and the rules resulting from the MST with NAR rule scheme

```
% add query subsumption rule
% add set-based rules, no rule variants

% query-generating rules with query pattern for negation
q(P) ==> copy(P,single(X)) | q(married(X)), q(person(X)).

% repair rule from NAR
repair @ married(X) \ single(X) <=> true.

% query-filtered rule from NAR without negation
apply @ q(P),person(X) ==> match(P,single(X)) | single(X).

% rules for DL facts
q(P) ==> match(P,person(sue)) | person(sue).
q(P) ==> match(P,person(sam)) | person(sam).
q(P) ==> match(P,married(sam)) | married(sam).
q(P) ==> match(P,married(fred)) | married(fred).
```

Here are some queries and their results.

```
?- q(married(sue)).
q(married(sue))
```

The query asks if sue is married. There is no fact in the database that matches the pattern `q(married(sue))` and no rule that derives facts for `married` is applicable. So the query will not derive any new facts, which means that `sue` is not married.

```
?- q(married(_)).
q(married(_)), married(fred), married(sam)
```

The query asks who is known to be married. The facts `married(fred)` and `married(sam)` are found in the database by applying the query-filtered rules for database facts and are returned as part of the answer.

```
?- q(single(_)).
q(married(_)), q(person(_)), q(single(_)),
person(sam), person(sue), married(fred), married(sam),
single(sue)
```

The query asks who is known to be single. It leads to the derivation of all facts for `person` and `married` caused by the MST query-generating rule because they are relevant to determining the single people. The corresponding MST query-filtered rule produces a fact `single` for each person. Then, the NAR repair rule will remove `single` if the person is married. Hence only the derived fact `single(sue)` stays in the answer, since according to the database `sue` is a person and not married.

15.6 Embedding CHR Subset in DL

Since DL does not have removal of atoms, only CHR programs implementing propagation algorithms with set-based constraints (like transitive closure) can be embedded in DL [64]. Concretely, CHR PGR propagation rules over a finite set of constants without built-ins and without guards can be directly written as DL inference rule.

15.7 Comparison DL and CHR

Datalog (DL) is a language to represent and query knowledge bases and databases. Unlike CHR and LA, DL uses nonmonotonic negation similar to negation-as-absence (NAA) from PR. For more sound reasoning, negation should be stratified and safe. We introduced *negation-as-repair (NAR)* for DL and generalized it for CHR PGR propagation rules with a single CHR constraint as body. Compared to NAA, the programs resulting from NAR are more concise and more declarative.

The semantics of DL is based on set-based bottom-up evaluation like Logical Algorithms (LA). Because terms are restricted to a finite set of constants, DL is decidable. The Magic Set Transformation (MST) simulates top-down evaluation using the bottom-up evaluation in DL. In the CHR embedding we can implement MST together with NAR in a more general way for CHR PGR propagation rules and with patterns that allow for variables. A restricted class of PGR propagation rules with set-based semantics can be embedded in DL.

15.8 Exercises DL

Exercise 16: PR Minimum with Negation in DL with NAR

Consider the rule for minimum from PR as DL rule

```
min(X) :- num(X), not((num(Y),Y<X)).
```

This rule makes use of a variable Y in the negation that violates range-restrictedness because is not mentioned in the positive part of the rule. Check if the CHR embedding of the rule with Negation-as-Repair (NAR) works. Compare the resulting code to the rules for minimum from the CHR introduction section and from GAMMA.

Exercise 17: PR Barber Paradox in DL with MST and NAR

Embed the DL version of Russell's Paradox in CHR using NAR.

```
man(X), -(shaves(X,X),true) ==> shaves(barber,X).
```

Consider again the four queries man(joe) and man(tim), shaves(tim,tim) as well as man(barber) and man(barber), shaves(barber,barber). The queries must now be extended with a query pattern q(shaves(_,_)) to find out who shaves whom. Describe the evaluations and their results and compare the results with those from the PR version.

Now embed the paradox in CHR using the DL Multi Set Transformation (MST) together with NAR. Consider the same queries again and compare the results with those of the previous version without MST.

Selected Solutions

PR Minimum with Negation in DL with NAR

```
% add set-basedness rules, no rule variants
num(X) \ num(X) <=> true.
min(X) \ min(X) <=> true.

% rules for NAR
repair @ num(Y) \ min(X) <=> Y<X | true : 0.
apply  @ num(X) ==> min(X) : 1.
```

PR Barber Paradox in DL with MST and NAR

```
% query subsumption rule
q(P1) \ q(P2) <=> match(P1,P2) | true.

% add set-based rules, no non-redundant rule variants
man(A) \ man(A) <=> true.
shaves(A,B) \ shaves(A,B) <=> true.

% query-generating rules with query pattern for negation
q(P) ==> copy(P,shaves(barber,X)) |
                        q(shaves(X,X)), q(man(X)).

% repair rule from NAR
repair @ shaves(X,X) \ shaves(barber,X) <=> true.

% query-filtered rule
apply @ q(P), man(X) ==> match(P,shaves(barber,X)) |
         shaves(barber,X).
```

Part IV

RULE-BASED PROGRAMMING

Rule-based programming languages include *Functional Programming (FP)*, that we already have derived from Term Rewriting Systems (TRS), and logic-based languages such as Constraint Logic Programming (CLP) and Concurrent Constraint Programming (CCP). Both employ logical inference in the form of if-then rules and constraint solving to perform computations. We will discuss in this part:

- *Constraint Logic Programming (CLP)* is a logic-based programming language. It uses top-down evaluation with built-in search for clauses with built-in constraints and built-in search where rules are clauses. It is a generalization of Prolog.

- *Concurrent Constraint Programming (CCP)* is a programming language with rules to express the behavior of systems where concurrently executing processes communicate by placing and checking constraints on shared variables.

Chapter 16

Constraint Logic Programming (CLP)

Logic Programming [71, 55] is a programming and knowledge representation paradigm based on formal logic. A logic program consists of a set of clauses, expressing facts and rules about some problem domain. *Prolog* is one of the most well-known languages for logic programming. It was conceived at the beginning of the 1970s. Logic Programming is typically applied in artificial intelligence (AI), such as expert systems, knowledge bases (databases), natural language processing (computational linguistics), computer vision, theorem proving and machine learning.

Constraint logic programming (CLP) [56, 38, 62] integrates constraint solving into logic programming. Constraint solving means solving problems by stating constraints (conditions, restrictions) that have to be satisfied by a solution and combining, simplifying and solving these constraints to narrow the search space before trying alternatives. Efficient special-purpose algorithms are employed to solve and simplify constraints. CLP has been applied in solving combinatorial optimization problems, in areas such as automated scheduling, type inference, civil engineering, mechanical engineering, digital circuit verification, air traffic control, and finance. The logic programming language *Prolog* can be understood an instance of CLP where the only built-in constraint is syntactic equality. *Datalog (DL)* in turn is a syntactic subset of Prolog without built-ins and where terms are restricted to a finite set of constants. Because DL is decidable, it does not qualify as a general-purpose programming language.

16.1 CLP Syntax and Semantics

Def. 16.1.1 (CLP Syntax) A *CLP program* is a set of *CLP clauses*

$$A \leftarrow B$$

where A is single atom and B is conjunction of atoms, built-ins and negated conjunctions of the form $neg(H)$ where H is a conjunction of atoms. All variables of a negated goal must also occur positively in the rule body (a case of range restriction). A CLP fact A is is shorthand for a clause $A \leftarrow true$. ∎

CLP clauses correspond to a specific form of logical implication that have a single head atom and a conjunction of atoms in the body. The head atom represents the conclusion of the rule, and the body atoms represent the conditions that must be satisfied for the rule to be true. A fact is represented by a clause with the fact as head atom and the body *true*.

16.1.1 Operational Semantics

A key characteristic of CLP is its *top-down evaluation strategy*, which is in contrast to *bottom-up evaluation* used in approaches with logical inference rules, Datalog (DL) and Logical Algorithms (LA). In *top-down evaluation*, the program starts with an initial goal (query) and tries to find a proof for it by applying clauses in the program. If a proof cannot be found, the evaluation *backtracks*, which means that it systematically tries the remaining clauses. This means that there may be multiple answers to a query.

The semantics of CLP is given by a state transition system.

Def. 16.1.2 (CLP Operational Semantics) A CLP *state* $\langle G, C \rangle$ is a pair of a goal (store) G and constraint (store) C. A CLP *initial state* is of the form $\langle G, true \rangle$ where G is called a CLP *query*. A *successful final state* is of the form $\langle true, C \rangle$ where C is different from *false*. A *failed final state* is of the form $\langle G, false \rangle$.

The transitions are:

Apply
If A is an atom, $(B \leftarrow H)$ is a copy of a clause in P
and $\mathcal{CT} \models \exists ((B \doteq A) \wedge C)$
then $\langle A \wedge G, C \rangle \mapsto \langle H \wedge G, (B \doteq A) \wedge C \rangle$
Fail
If A is an atom to which no clause is applicable
then $\langle A \wedge G, C \rangle \mapsto \langle G, false \rangle$
Solve
If $\mathcal{CT} \models \forall ((C \wedge D_1) \leftrightarrow D_2)$, C is a built-in constraint
then $\langle C \wedge G, D_1 \rangle \mapsto \langle G, D_2 \rangle$
where $\mathcal{CT}$ is a logical theory describing the built-in constraints. ∎

The **Apply** transition behaves as follows: If the syntactic equation between head of the clause and the selected atom is consistent with the current constraint store, then the atom is replaced by the body of the clause and the equality is added to the constraint store. Otherwise, if no clause is applicable to the selected atom, the computation fails due to the **Fail** transition. If a built-in constraint was selected, then the **Solve** transition will move it from the goal store to the constraint store that is simplified in the process.

All clauses are tried for the selected atom. This backtrack search for clause choices in the **Apply** step is left implicit in the state transition system. Backtracking in logic programming systematically explores all combinations of clause choices. It starts by selecting the first clause for the selected goal. Each clause choice is recorded as a choice point. Then it recursively continues with the new goals added by the chosen clause. If a goal leads to a failed state, the algorithm backtracks to the previous choice point and selects the next applicable clause. This process continues until all possible clause combinations have been explored or a successful final state is reached.

16.1.2 CLP Negation-as-Failure (NAF)

CLP features nonmonotonic *negation-as-failure (NAF)*, which is similar to negation-as-absence (NAA) from Production Rules (PR) and negation-as-repair (NAF) from Datalog (DL). In NAF, negation of a goal holds if it cannot be derived while checking the negation. All these concepts of negation are based on the *closed-world assumption (CWA)*.

In order to use NAF for more sound reasoning, negation must be safe. As in DL, safeness holds if the negated atom is ground at the time of execution. This is ensured by the syntactic condition that all variables of a negated goal must also occur positively in the rule body.

Def. 16.1.3 (CLP Negation-as-Failure (NAF))　　We add the following transition to the CLP semantics.

> **Negate**
> If　　　　$\langle A, C \rangle \mapsto^* \langle true, D \rangle$, $D \neq false$
> then　　　$\langle neg(A) \wedge G, C \rangle \mapsto \langle G, false \rangle$
> else　　　$\langle neg(A) \wedge G, C \rangle \mapsto \langle G, C \rangle$
> ∎

In the **Negate** transition, the computation fails if the computation with the negated goal leads to a successful final state. Otherwise the computation is continued with the remainder of the goal.

16.1.3 Declarative Semantics

Clark's completion defines the declarative semantics of a Constraint Logic Programming (CLP) program as a logic formula according to the closed-world assumption (CWA). Any predicate that cannot be proven to hold is assumed to be false.

Def. 16.1.4 (CLP Declarative Semantics) *Clark's completion* of a CLP program is defined as follows. For each predicate p/n occurring in a given CLP program, defined by m clauses

$$\bigwedge_{i=1}^{m} \forall (p(\bar{t}_i) \leftarrow G_i),$$

we add the first-order logic formula

$$p(\bar{x}) \leftrightarrow \bigvee_{i=1}^{m} \exists \bar{y}_i \ (\bar{t}_i = \bar{x} \wedge G_i)$$

where $\bar{t}_i$ is a sequence of n terms, $\bar{y}_i$ are the variables in G_i and t_i, and $\bar{x}$ is a sequence of n new variables. $\blacksquare$

Clark's completion of a predicate expresses the logical equivalence between a predicate and the clauses that define it. The right-hand side of the formula is a disjunction, each disjunct corresponding to a clause of the predicate.

16.2 Magic Set Transformation with Negation-as-Repair for CLP in CHR

Prolog and CLP programs are translated into CHR$^\vee$ in [7] based on Clark's completion. CHR$^\vee$ extends CHR by disjunction in the body of CHR rules. The disjuncts are explored by backtrack search as in Prolog. This embedding of a CLP program considers each predicate as a CHR constraint and represents Clark's completion as CHR$^\vee$ simplification rules with disjunction.

Here we want to rely on standard CHR without extensions. We could implement disjunction with a meta-interpreter that evaluates each disjunct on its own until one that does not fail is found. As we prefer straightforward source-to-source transformation and as we already have the means, we use an extended variant of Datalog Magic Set Transformation (DL MST) with negation-as-repair (NAR). It requires for stratified and safe negation. It changes the semantics of CLP somewhat, since it computes all answers bottom-up at once and keeps intermediate results.

Def. 16.2.1 (Rule Scheme for CLP with MST and NAR)
The *query pattern subsumption rule* comes first in the program

```
subsume @ q(P1) \ q(P2) ⇔ match(P1,P2) | true,
```

where P1 and P2 are variables.

Each CLP clause of a program with stratified and safe negation

B ← C ∧ H1...Hn ∧ neg(NH1,NC1)...neg(NHm,NCm)

where B is an atom, C is a possibly empty conjunction of the built-ins, H1...Hn is a possibly empty conjunction of atoms and neg(NH1,NC1)...neg(NHm,NCm) is a possibly empty conjunction of negated pairs of atoms and built-in constraints with stratified negation, translates to CHR rules

```
% MST query-generating rule with negation (if not n=m=0)
N @ q(P) ⇒ C ∧ copy(P,B) | q(NH1)...q(NHm) ∧ q(H1)...q(Hn)

% repair rules for negation with NAR
repair-N @ NH1 \ B ⇔ NC1 | true
...
repair-N @ NHm \ B ⇔ NCm | true

% MST query-filtered rule without negation
apply-N @ q(P) ∧ H1...Hn ⇒ C ∧ copy(P,B) | B
```

To the translated rules we add the derived rule variants from the set-based transformation of LA (Definition 14.3.2).

In a query, the CLP atoms are turned into query patterns by wrapping them with q/1. ∎

Query-generating rules are only produced for clauses that have at least one atom in the body. Note that unlike MST for DL, in CLP copy/2 instead of match/2 is needed for query-filtered rules because the derived atom B may not be ground during computation.

Examples CLP MST in CHR

The next examples illustrate the use of MST for CLP in CHR.

Example 16.2.1 (CLP Minimum in CHR with MST) The minimum predicate compares two numbers and returns the smaller one.

```
min(X,Y,X) :- X=<Y.
min(X,Y,Y) :- X>=Y.
```

The CLP clauses are transformed into query-filtered rules in CHR. There are no query-generating rules, because the body of the clauses contain only built-ins.

```
% add set-based rules
% query-filtered rules
q(P) ==> copy(P,min(X,Y,X)),X=<Y | min(X,Y,X).
q(P) ==> copy(P,min(X,Y,Y)),X>=Y | min(X,Y,Y).
```

Some sample queries and their answers are discussed below:

```
?- q(min(1,2,_)).
   q(min(1,2,_)), min(1,2,1)
```

So the minimum of 1 and 2 is 1.

```
?- q(min(1,1,_)).
   q(min(1,1,_)), min(1,1,1), min(1,1,1)
```

We get two identical answers, because both clauses apply and have the same result. There is no set-basedness in CLP.

```
?- q(min(1,0,1)).
   q(min(1,0,1))
```

No answer is produced, this means the CLP computation fails because there is no clause that applies to the query.

Example 16.2.2 (CLP Append in CHR with MST) This is a classical Prolog predicate over three lists which holds if the concatenation of the first and second list equals the third list. The program for **append/3** has two clauses, one for the case where the first list is empty and the other where the first list is non-empty.

```
append([],L,L).
append([H|L1],L2,[H|L3]) :- append(L1,L2,L3).
```

The fact states that when the first list is empty, the second list is the resulting list. The rule states that the concatenation of list with a head H and a second list is a list with the same head H and a tail that is the result of concatenating the tail of the first list with the second list. MST replaces the clauses for append with two sets of CHR rules, the query-generating rules and the query-filtered rules.

```
% query-generating rules (not for facts)
q(P) ==> copy(P,append([B|C],D,[B|E])) | q(append(C,D,E)).
```

```
% query-filtered rules
q(P) ==> copy(P,append([],B,B)) | append([],B,B).
q(P), append(C,D,E) ==> copy(P,append([B|C],D,[B|E])) |
      append([B|C],D,[B|E]).
```

Some sample queries and their answers are discussed below.

```
?- q(append(a,_,_)).
q(append(a,_,_))
```

The query q(append(a,_,_)) fails to produce any answer because there is no clause that applies to that query.

```
?- q(append([1],[2],L)).
q(append([1],[2],_)), q(append([],[2],_))
append([1],[2],[1,2]), append([],[2],[2])
```

The query q(append([1],[2],L)) yields append([1],[2],[1,2]) and append([],[2],[2]) as the answers.

```
?- q(append(L1,L2,[1,2])).
q(append(_,_,[1,2])),q(append(_,_,[2])),q(append(_,_,[])),
append([],[1,2],[1,2]), append([1],[2],[1,2]),
append([1,2],[],[1,2]), append([],[2],[2]),
append([2],[],[2]), append([],[],[])
```

The query q(append(L1,L2,[1,2])) produces multiple answers, showing all the possible ways that two lists can be concatenated to produce the list [1,2].

Finally, the query q(append(L1,L2,L3)) does not terminate because there are infinitely many ways that arbitrary lists can be concatenated.

16.3 Embedding CHR Subset in CLP

CHR cannot be embedded in pure Prolog [43], but approximated in CLP [48]. For a semantically equivalent embedding, only single-headed CHR simplification rules can be directly represented as CLP rules provided the CHR program is confluent and provided any computation in the program ends in a final state that does not contain CHR constraints, but only built-in constraints.

16.4 Comparison CLP and CHR

Like CHR, the rule-based CLP does have logical variables subjected to built-in constraints. This allows for non-ground computations. Unlike CHR, CLP does not feature multiple head atoms.

CLP features backtrack search to systematically explore all possible clause choices. CHR does not have built-in search, but it can be provided by an extension that introduces disjunction, $CHR^{\vee}$.

Unlike CHR, CLP features nonmonotonic *negation-as-failure (NAF)*, which is similar to negation-as-absence (NAA) from Production Rules (PR) and negation-as-repair (NAF) from Datalog (DL). In NAA and NAR we check for absence of a fact, while in NAF we try to derive the negated facts top-down during checking negation.

We embedded CLP with stratified and safe negation in CHR without search by using the Magic Set Transformation (MST) with Negation-as-Repair (NAR) from DL. This changes the semantics of CLP from top-down to bottom-up computation. CLP can embed single-headed CHR simplification rules of confluent CHR programs whose final states only contain built-in constraints.

16.5 Exercises CLP

Exercise 18: Fibonacci Numbers

Implement the Fibonacci numbers in CLP and translate the resulting program into CHR using MST. Compare it to the CHR versions of the problem.

Exercise 19: Remove List Element

The CLP predicate **remove** holds if the removal of the first argument from the list in the second argument results in the list in the third argument. Translate the CLP program into CHR. Give some sample queries and explain their answers.

```
remove(X, [X|Xs], Xs).
remove(X, [Y|Xs], [Y|Xs1]) :-
          remove(X, Xs, Xs1).
```

Exercise 20: Transitive Closure

Interpret the DL transitive closure program as CLP program.
```
p(X,Y) :- e(X,Y).
p(X,Z) :- e(X,Y), p(Y,Z).
```

Assume that given edges are provided as CLP facts. Pose some sample queries for paths. How is the termination behavior of the CLP program?

Chapter 17

Concurrent Constraint Programming (CCP)

Concurrent Constraint Programming (CCP) [63] is a constraint programming framework that allows for concurrent and parallel execution. Rules express the behavior of concurrently executing processes that communicate by placing and checking constraints on shared variables. The languages of CCP are the ones closest to CHR. We consider here the search-free fragment of the CCP language framework.

17.1 CCP Syntax and Semantics

A CC program consists of predicate declarations.

Def. 17.1.1 (CCP Syntax) A CC program consists of a set of *declarations* of the form

$$p(\tilde{t}) \leftarrow A,$$

where p/n is a predicate symbol and $\tilde{t}$ stands for a sequence of n terms forming the arguments of p. Each predicate p is defined by exactly one declaration. The body of a declaration D is an agent A.

An *agent* A is a parallel composition $\parallel$ of constraints, agents and case expressions. A *case expression* consists of the sum $\sum_{i=1}^{n}$ of cases each written as $c_i \rightarrow A_i$ where c_i is a condition and A_i is an Agent. ∎

The *operational semantics* of CCP is described by a transition system.

Def. 17.1.2 (CCP Operational Semantics) CCP states $\langle A, c \rangle$ are pairs of an agent A and the constraint store c. The transitions are as follows.

Apply

$$\langle p(\bar{t}), c \rangle \mapsto \langle A, \bar{t}{=}\bar{s} \wedge c \rangle \text{ if a declaration } p(\bar{s}) \leftarrow A \text{ is in program } P$$

Ask

$$\langle \sum_{i=1}^{n} c_i \rightarrow A_i, d \rangle \mapsto \langle A_j, d \rangle \text{ if } CT \models \forall(d \rightarrow c_j) \ (1 \leq j \leq n)$$

Tell

$$\langle c, d \rangle \mapsto \langle true, d' \rangle \text{ if } CT \models \forall(c \wedge d \leftrightarrow d')$$

Compose

$$\frac{\langle A, c \rangle \mapsto \langle A', c' \rangle}{\begin{array}{l} \langle (A \parallel B), c \rangle \mapsto \langle (A' \parallel B), c' \rangle \\ \langle (B \parallel A), c \rangle \mapsto \langle (B \parallel A'), c' \rangle \end{array}}$$

∎

Transition **Apply** replaces an agent $p(\bar{t})$ by its definition according to its declaration. Note that $\bar{t}{=}\bar{s}$ means that syntactic equality, not matching, is used for parameter passing. The concurrent communication mechanism of CCP is based on the ask-and-tell metaphor. The **Ask** transition checks whether a constraint is logically implied by the current constraint store. The **Tell** transition imposes a constraint by adding it to the constraint store (like the **Solve** transition in CLP). In the case expression $\sum_{i=1}^{n} c_i \rightarrow A_i$, **Ask** nondeterministically chooses a constraint c_i which is implied by the current constraint store d, and continues computation with the corresponding agent A_i. In transition **Compose**, concurrent computation is defined using a interleaving semantics, i.e. by interleaving sequential computations steps of agents.

17.2 Embedding CCP in CHR

CCP predicates are embedded as CHR constraints and CCP constraints are embedded as built-in constraints. CCP declarations and Ask operations are translated into CHR simplification rules.

Def. 17.2.1 (Rule Scheme for CCP) Each CCP declaration

$$p(\tilde{t}) \leftarrow A$$

is replaced by the CHR simplification rule

$$p(\tilde{x}) \Leftrightarrow \bar{x} = \bar{s} \wedge A,$$

where $\tilde{x}$ is a sequence of new variables.

CCP agents are translated into CHR goals where composition $\|$ is replaced by conjunction $\wedge$ in CHR.

Each case expression $\sum_{i=1}^{n} c_i \rightarrow A_i$ of a given CC program is wrapped by the auxiliary CHR constraint `ask/1` and n simplification rules of the form

$$\text{ask}(\sum_{i=1}^{n} c_i \rightarrow A_i) \Leftrightarrow c_i \mid A_i \ \ (1 \leq i \leq n)$$

are added to the embedding. ∎

The case expression of the Ask operation is embedded as a set of simplification rules, one for each case.

Example CCP in CHR

Example 17.2.1 (Minimum in CCP) The minimum relation can be implemented in CCP as the agent

```
min(X,Y,Z) ← (X=<Y→X=Z)+(Y=<X→Y=Z)
```

The embedding into CHR gives

```
min(A,B,C) <=>
    [A,B,C]=[X,Y,Z], ask((X=<Y->X=Z)+(Y=<X->Y=Z)).

ask((X=<Y->X=Z)+(Y=<X->Y=Z)) <=> X=<Y | X=Z.
ask((X=<Y->X=Z)+(Y=<X->Y=Z)) <=> Y=<X | Y=Z.
```

17.3 Embedding CHR Subset in CCP

CCP can express CHR simplification rules with single head constraints using case expressions instead of guards.

Def. 17.3.1 (CHR Subset in CCP) For each constraint c/n occurring in a given CHR program, defined by m simplification rules with single head constraints

$$c(\bar{t}_i) \Leftrightarrow C_i \mid B_i,$$

the embedding in CCP adds the declaration for the predicate c/n

$$c(\bar{x}) \leftarrow \sum_{i=1}^{m} (\bar{t}_i = \bar{x} \wedge C_i \rightarrow B_i'),$$

where $\bar{t}_i$ is a sequence of n terms, $\bar{x}$ is a sequence of n new variables and where B_i' is the result of replacing each conjunction by the parallel composition operator in B_i. ∎

17.4 Comparison CCP and CHR

Like CHR, the rule-based programming languages CLP and CCP have logical variables subjected to built-in constraints. This allows for non-ground computations in these programming languages. Unlike CHR, CLP and CCP do not feature multiple head atoms. The full CCP framework features search, which is not present in CHR without extensions. CCP can be embedded in CHR using single-headed simplification rules for declarations and case expressions. CCP can embed CHR simplification rules with single head constraints.

17.5 Exercises CCP

Exercise 21: CCP Hamming Numbers Problem in CHR

Consider the classical Hamming Problem, which is to compute an ordered ascending sequence of all numbers whose only prime factors are 2, 3 or 5. The sequence starts with the numbers

$1, 2, 3, 4, 5, 6, 8, 9, 10, 12, 15, 16, 18, 20, 24, 25, \ldots$. The idea for solving this problem is based on the observation that any element of the sequence (except for the first number 1) can be obtained by multiplying a previous number of the sequence with 2, 3 or 5. Assuming that we already know the sequence, we can thus reconstruct it by multiplying every number in it by 2, 3 and 5, respectively, and by merging the resulting three sequences without duplicates. The following CC program produces the infinite list of Hamming numbers.

```
hamming(S) <- S1=[1|S] ||
   mults(S1,2,S2) || mults(S1,3,S3) || mults(S1,5,S5)) ||
   merge(S2,S3,S23) || merge(S5,S23,S).

mults(S,N,L) <-
             S=[X|Xs]->(L=[X*N|XsN] || mults(Xs,N,XsN)).

merge(L1,L2,L3) <- (L1=[X|Xs] || L2=[Y|Ys]) ->
           ( (X=Y->(L3=[X|Out] || merge(Xs,Ys,Out))
           + (X<Y->(L3=[X|Out] || merge(Xs,[Y|Ys],Out))
           + (X>Y->(L3=[Y|Out] || merge([X|Xs],Ys,Out))).

observe(L) <- (L=[X|Xs] || number(X)) ->
                       (write(X) || blank || observe(Xs)).
```

The query to produce the Hamming numbers sequence is `observe(S)` || `hamming(S)`. The predicate `observe/1` serves as an observer agent. It takes the list of Hamming numbers as arguments. Whenever the next number in the list is known, it outputs the number followed by a blank and recursively proceeds to observe the tail of the list.

Embed this CC program in CHR.

Chapter 18

Summary: Rule-based Approaches in CHR

This book introduced a comprehensive variety of rule-based formalisms, systems, and programming languages. The expressiveness, effectiveness and efficiency of CHR enabled the high-level embedding of the characteristic features of these rule-based approaches in CHR by straightforward source-to-source translation.

We first described the CHR programming language and its properties. The rule-based formalisms discussed were General Abstract Model for Multiset Manipulation (GAMMA), Term Rewriting Systems (TRS), and Colored Petri Nets (CPN). These formalisms use rewrite rules to transform terms or graphs. We also introduced Functional Programming (FP) languages like Haskell under the heading of formalisms because FP can be derived from TRS.

The rule-based systems discussed were Production Rules (PR) like OPS5 and Drools, and its extension Event-Condition-Action (ECA) Rules as well as Logical Algorithms (LA) and Datalog (DL) that are based on bottom-up evaluation of inference rules. These systems use a set of rules to describe how to transform data facts.

The rule-based programming languages included the aforementioned Functional Programming (FP) as well as Constraint Logic Programming (CLP) like Prolog (a superset of DL) and Concurrent Constraint Programming (CCP). These programming paradigms rely on constraint solving for computation.

The unique combination of features in CHR enables advanced high-level rule-based programming, making it an ideal platform for embedding other rule-based approaches. On the other hand embedding the full functionality of CHR into other rule-based approaches is challenging due to the inherent differences in expressiveness.

18.1 Embedding Rule-Based Approaches in CHR

We have shown how to implement typical features of other rule-based approaches that are missing in CHR with simple rule schemes. Some features have also been provided as language extensions of CHR in the literature.

- Unlike rule-based systems, CHR has no built-in *conflict resolution* for choosing rules for application in an explicit way except for rule order under its refined semantics. Related extensions of CHR by *rule priorities* [54] and by rules with *probabilities* [39, 19, 66] exist.

- CHR has a *multiset-based semantics*, while LA and DL have a *set-based semantics*. In [53] an embedding of the Logical Algorithms (LA) language into CHR with set-based semantics, *permanent deletion* and *rule priorities* is given, and also a translation of rules with priorities into regular CHR.

- Unlike rule-based systems, CHR does not have the verbose *explicit deletion and explicit insertion* of facts, but it can be easily provided.

- CHR does not provide for *negation* because its nonmonotonicity causes semantic problems, while negation-as-failure exists in CLP and negation-as-absence in rule-based systems. CHR extended with negation-as-absence is defined and implemented in [75]. We also introduced negation-as-repair (NAR) from DL in CHR.

164

- *Bottom-up* and *top-down* evaluation were combined by the *magic set transformation* of DL that we generalized for CHR and also applied to CLP.

- Unlike CLP, CHR does not have *built-in search*, but the extension of CHR$^\vee$ has disjunction [7] and extending CHR with advanced search routines has also been proposed [78, 21].

- Another noteworthy extension not covered in this book is adaptive CHR [77, 36], where CHR constraints and their consequences can be retracted dynamically using justifications. These works support more sound *nonmonotonic reasoning*.

Chapter 6 of our book [31] sketches some embeddings of rule-based approaches in CHR. In addition, in Chapter 9.3 of the book, description logic (DL) with OWL- and SWRL-style rules for the semantic web is embedded in CHR.

18.2 Embedding CHR in other Rule-Based Approaches

In this section, we explore the key features of CHR and which of them can be embedded into other rule-based approaches.

One of the distinguishing features of CHR is its ability to handle *logical variables*, which can be subjected to built-in constraints. This allows computation with partial or unknown information (i.e., non-ground constraints). Only logic-based programming languages, such as Constraint Logic Programming (CLP) and Concurrent Constraint Programming (CCP), support logical variables and enable computation with non-ground constraints. Furthermore, guard checking as logical implication is a feature that is only available in CCP.

In contrast, rule-based formalisms and systems rely on a *ground representation*, where logical variables cannot be represented. The *positive ground range-restricted (PGR) fragment* of CHR has range-restricted rules without failing built-ins in the body and only allows ground queries. In this way computations stay ground and do not fail.

CHR provides three types of rules: *simplification and simpagation rules*, which replace matched removable constraints, and *propagation rules*, which add new constraints without removing any existing ones. The rule-based formalisms and programming languages support only one type of rules in restricted forms.

CHR PGR rules can be embedded into rule-based systems Production Rules (PR), Event-Condition-Action (ECA) rules and Logical Algorithms (LA). Only set-based CHR PGR propagation rules over finite data without built-ins can be embedded in Datalog (DL). CHR PGR simplification and simpagation rules, but not propagation rules, can be embedded into the rule-based formalisms GAMMA and Colored Petri Nets (CPN).

A restricted form of *CHR simplification rules* that admits a functional notation can be embedded in Term Rewriting Systems (TRS) (without built-ins) and Functional Programming (FP). CHR simplification rules with only single head constraints can be embedded in CCP. A further restricted class of such rules in confluent CHR programs can be embedded in CLP. These embeddings are somewhat surprising since CLP and CCP are programming languages close to CHR, but can only embed a very small fragment of CHR rules. No rule-based approach that we have discussed can embed full CHR.

CHR performs computations justified by a *declarative semantics* which interprets rules as logical formulas. This declarative semantics is closely related to its operational semantics, providing a solid foundation for reasoning about the correctness of the rules. While some other rule-based formalisms and languages, such as TRS, FP, DL, and CLP, also provide declarative semantics, many other approaches lack this capability, making CHR particularly strong in terms of reasoning and formal verification.

18.3 Conclusions

What distinguishes CHR from other programming languages and formalisms is its combination of multiset transformation, propagation rules, logical variables, and built-in constraints into a logic-based efficient declarative language which admits powerful program analysis.

Effective and efficient high-level embeddings by source-to-source translation allow for straightforward integration of a comprehensive variety of rule-based approaches into CHR. Each approach has its own strengths and weaknesses. By embedding these approaches into CHR, it provides a common platform for execution and analysis of rule-based systems, formalisms, and languages.

Our embeddings allow for the use of the features and constructs of the embedded language within CHR. It enables to add new functionality to languages and to facilitate interoperability between different languages. CHR enables cross-fertilization of the approaches by the direct comparison based on their CHR implementations, and opens up possibilities for combining them in novel ways. In this way, CHR can serve as a unifying computational formalism, a lingua franca, across computer science.

Acknowledgements

I would like to thank my research and teaching assistants Hariolf Betz, Daniel Gall, Frank Raiser, Sascha Rechenberger and Amira Zaki as well as the active students of my regular courses on rule-based programming at Ulm University, and singular courses at German University in Cairo and Ca' Foscari University of Venice, during almost 20 years.

My thanks also go to the fellow researches who contributed so marvelously to the field of rule-based programming and to the Constraint Handling Rules language especially, for example at the numerous CHR workshops around the world. In particular, I thoroughly enjoyed the inspiring discussions with Jesper Larsson Träff and his suggestions for improvement for this book.

This book could not have been written without the sabbatical from Ulm University during the winter term 2024/25.

Bibliography

[1] S. Abdennadher. Operational semantics and confluence of constraint propagation rules. In G. Smolka, editor, *CP '97: Proc. Third Intl. Conf. Principles and Practice of Constraint Programming*, volume 1330 of *LNCS*, pages 252–266. SV, 1997.

[2] S. Abdennadher, G. Fakhry, and N. Sharaf. Towards the implementation of source-to-source transformation tool for CHR operational semantics. In G. Gupta, editor, *LOPSTR13*, 2013.

[3] S. Abdennadher and T. Frühwirth. On completion of constraint handling rules. In M. J. Maher and J.-F. Puget, editors, *CP98l*, volume 1520 of *LNCS*, pages 25–39. SV, October 1998.

[4] S. Abdennadher and T. Frühwirth. Operational equivalence of CHR programs and constraints. In J. Jaffar, editor, *CP99l*, volume 1713 of *LNCS*, pages 43–57. SV, October 1999.

[5] S. Abdennadher and T. Frühwirth. Integration and optimization of rule-based constraint solvers. In M. Bruynooghe, editor, *LOPSTR03*, volume 3018 of *LNCS*, pages 198–213. SV, 2004.

[6] S. Abdennadher, T. Frühwirth, and H. Meuss. Confluence and Semantics of Constraint Simplification Rules. *Constraints*, 4(2):133–165, 1999.

[7] S. Abdennadher and H. Schütz. CHRv: A Flexible Query Language. In *Third International Conference on Flexible Query Answering Systems*, volume 1495 of *Lecture Notes in Computer Science*, pages 1–14. Springer, 1998.

[8] F. Baader and T. Nipkow. *Term Rewriting and All That*. Cambridge University Press, 1998.

[9] J.-P. Banâtre, A. Coutant, and D. L. Metayer. A Parallel Machine for Multiset Transformation and its Programming Style. *Future Generation Computer Systems*, 4(2):133–144, 1988.

[10] J.-P. Banâtre and D. L. Métayer. Programming by Multiset Transformation. *Communications of the ACM*, 36(1):98–111, 1993.

[11] V. Barichard. CHR++: An efficient CHR system in c++ with don't know non-determinism. *Expert Systems with Applications*, 238:121810, 2024.

[12] L. Bellomarini, G. Gottlob, and E. Sallinger. The vadalog system: Datalog-based reasoning for knowledge graphs. *arXiv preprint arXiv:1807.08709*, 2018.

[13] G. Berry and G. Boudol. The Chemical Abstract Machine. *Theoretical Computer Science*, 96(1):217–248, 1992.

[14] B. Berstel, P. Bonnard, F. Bry, M. Eckert, and P.-L. Pătrânjan. Reactive rules on the web. *Reasoning Web: Third International Summer School 2007, Dresden, Germany, September 3-7, 2007, Tutorial Lectures 3*, pages 183–239, 2007.

[15] H. Betz. Relating Coloured Petri Nets to Constraint Handling Rules. In *Fourth Workshop on Constraint Handling Rules*, pages 32–46, 2007.

[16] L. Brownston, R. Farrell, E. Kant, and N. Martin. *Programming Expert Systems in OPS5: An Introduction to Rule-based Programming*. Addison-Wesley, Boston, MA, USA, 1985.

[17] S. Ceri, G. Gottlob, and L. Tanca. What You Always Wanted to Know About Datalog (And Never Dared to Ask). *IEEE Transaction on Knowledge and Data Engineering*, 1(1):146–166, 1989.

[18] B. Chin, D. von Dincklage, V. Ercegovac, P. Hawkins, M. S. Miller, F. Och, C. Olston, and F. Pereira. Yedalog: Exploring knowledge at scale. In *1st Summit on Advances in Programming Languages (SNAPL 2015)*. Schloss Dagstuhl-Leibniz-Zentrum fuer Informatik, 2015.

[19] H. Christiansen. Implementing probabilistic abductive logic programming with Constraint Handling Rules. In *Constraint Handling Rules*, pages 85–118. Springer, 2008.

[20] L. De Koninck. Logical algorithms meets CHR: A meta-complexity result for constraint handling rules with rule priorities. *TPLP*, 9(2):165–212, March 2009.

[21] L. De Koninck, T. Schrijvers, and B. Demoen. A flexible search framework for CHR. *Constraint Handling Rules: Current Research Topics*, pages 16–47, 2008.

[22] G. J. Duck, P. J. Stuckey, and S. Brand. ACD Term Rewriting. In *22nd International Conference on Logic Programming*, volume 4079 of *Lecture Notes in Computer Science*, pages 117–131. Springer, 2006.

[23] G. J. Duck, P. J. Stuckey, M. Garcia de la Banda, and C. Holzbaur. The refined operational semantics of constraint handling rules. In B. Demoen and V. Lifschitz, editors, *ICLP04l*, volume 3132 of *LNCS*, pages 90–104. SV, September 2004.

[24] G. J. Duck and M. Sulzmann, editors. *CHR 2007, Forth International Workshop on Constraint Handling Rules*, September 2007.

[25] A. Eisenberg and J. Melton. SQL: 1999, formerly known as SQL3. *ACM SIGMOD Record*, 28(1):131–138, 1999.

[26] E. Friedman-Hill. *Jess in Action*. Manning Publications, 2003.

[27] T. Frühwirth. Proving Termination of Constraint Solver Programs. In *Selected Papers from the Joint ERCIM/Compulog Net Workshop on New Trends in Contraints*, volume 1865 of *Lecture Notes in Computer Science*, pages 298–317. Springer, 2000.

[28] T. Frühwirth. As Time Goes By: Automatic Complexity Analysis of Simplification Rules. In *Eighth International Conference on Principles of Knowledge Representation and Reasoning*, San Francisco, CA, USA, 2002. Morgan Kaufmann.

[29] T. Frühwirth. As Time Goes By II: More Automatic Complexity Analysis of Concurrent Rule Programs. *Electronic Notes in Theoretical Computer Science*, 59(3):185–206, 2002.

[30] T. Frühwirth. Specialization of concurrent guarded multi-set transformation rules. In S. Etalle, editor, *LOPSTR04*, volume 3573 of *LNCS*, pages 133–148. SV, 2005.

[31] T. Frühwirth. *Constraint handling rules.* Cambridge University Press, 2009.

[32] T. Frühwirth. Constraint handling rules - what else? In *Rule Technologies: Foundations, Tools, and Applications - 9th International Symposium, RuleML 2015, Berlin, Germany, August 2-5, 2015, Proceedings*, pages 13–34, 2015.

[33] T. Frühwirth. A devil's advocate against termination of direct recursion. In *17th International Symposium on Principles and Practice of Declarative Programming, PPDP '15, Siena, Italy, 2015.* ACM, 2015.

[34] T. Frühwirth. Parallelism, concurrency and distribution in constraint handling rules: A survey. *Theory and Practice of Logic Programming*, 18(5-6):759–805, 2018.

[35] T. Frühwirth. *The Computer Art of Mason's Mark Design with VanDeGraphGenerator.* BoD, 2018.

[36] T. Frühwirth. Justifications in constraint handling rules for logical retraction in dynamic algorithms: Theory, implementations, and complexity. *Fundamenta Informaticae*, 173(4):253–283, 2020.

[37] T. Frühwirth. Runtime repeated recursion unfolding: A just-in-time online program optimization that can achieve super-linear

speedup. *arXiv preprint arXiv:2307.02180, submitted to Fundamenta Informaticae*, 2024.

[38] T. Frühwirth and S. Abdennadher. *Essentials of Constraint Programming*. Springer, 2003.

[39] T. Frühwirth, A. di Pierro, and H. Wiklicky. Probabilistic Constraint Handling Rules. In *11th International Workshop on Functional and (Constraint) Logic Programming*, volume 76 of *Electronic Notes in Theoretical Computer Science*, pages 115–130, 2002.

[40] T. Frühwirth and C. Holzbaur. Source-to-source transformation for a class of expressive rules. In F. Buccafurri, editor, *AGP '03: Joint Conf. Declarative Programming APPIA-GULP-PRODE*, pages 386–397, September 2003.

[41] T. Frühwirth and E. Kühn. VIP—DBS ein integriertes logikorientiertes datenbank management system unter VIP-Prolog. In *Die Zukunft der Informationssysteme Lehren der 80er Jahre: Dritte gemeinsame Fachtagung der Österreichischen Gesellschaft für Informatik (ÖGI) und der Gesellschaft für Informatik (GI) Johannes Kepler Universität Linz*, pages 253–264. Springer, 1986.

[42] T. Frühwirth and F. Raiser, editors. *Constraint Handling Rules: Compilation, Execution, and Analysis*. BoD, March 2011.

[43] M. Gabbrielli, J. Mauro, and M. C. Meo. The expressive power of CHR with priorities. *Inf. Comput.*, 228:62–82, 2013.

[44] M. Gabbrielli, M. C. Meo, P. Tacchella, and H. Wiklicky. Unfolding for chr programs. *Theory and Practice of Logic Programming*, 15(3):264–311, 2015.

[45] H. Ganzinger and D. M. Allester. A New Meta-Complexity Theorem for Bottom-Up Logic Programs. In *First International Joint Conference on Automated Reasoning*, volume 2083 of *Lecture Notes in Computer Science*, pages 514–528. Springer, 2001.

[46] H. Ganzinger and D. McAllester. Logical Algorithms. In *18th International Conference on Logic Programming*, volume 2401 of *Lecture Notes in Computer Science*, pages 31–42. Springer, 2002.

[47] J. C. Giarratano and G. Riley. *Expert Systems: Principles and Programming*. PWS Publishing Co., Boston, MA, USA, 1994.

[48] R. Haemmerle, P. Lopez-Garcia, and M. Hermenegildo. Clp projection for constraint handling rules. In M. Hanus, editor, *PPDP11*, pages 137–148. ACM, July 2011.

[49] C. Holzbaur and T. Frühwirth. A prolog constraint handling rules compiler and runtime system. In C. Holzbaur and T. Frühwirth, editors, *Special Issue on Constraint Handling Rules*, volume 14(4) of *Journal of Applied Artificial Intelligence*, pages 369–388. Taylor and Francis, April 2000.

[50] C. Holzbaur, M. Garcia de la Banda, P. J. Stuckey, and G. J. Duck. Optimizing compilation of constraint handling rules in hal. In S. Abdennadher, T. Frühwirth, and C. Holzbaur, editors, *Special Issue on Constraint Handling Rules*, volume 5(4–5) of *Theory and Practice of Logic Programming*, pages 503–531. CUP, July 2005.

[51] P. Hudak. Conception, evolution, and application of functional programming languages. *ACM Computing Surveys (CSUR)*, 21(3):359–411, 1989.

[52] G. Hutton. *Programming in Haskell*. Cambridge University Press, 2016.

[53] L. D. Koninck, T. Schrijvers, and B. Demoen. The Correspondence Between the Logical Algorithms Language and CHR. In *23rd International Conference on Logic Programming*, volume 4670 of *Lecture Notes in Computer Science*, pages 209–223. Springer, 2007.

[54] L. D. Koninck, T. Schrijvers, and B. Demoen. User-definable Rule Priorities for CHR. In *Ninth ACM SIGPLAN International Con-*

ference on Principles and Practice of Declarative Programming, pages 25–36. ACM, 2007.

[55] R. Kowalski. *Logic for Problem Solving, Revisited.* Computer Science Essentials. Books on Demand, 2014.

[56] K. Marriott and P. J. Stuckey. *Programming with Constraints : An Introduction.* MIT Press, 1998.

[57] F. Nogatz, T. Frühwirth, and D. Seipel. CHR. js: A CHR implementation in javascript. In *Rules and Reasoning: Second International Joint Conference, RuleML+ RR 2018, Luxembourg, Luxembourg, September 18–21, 2018, Proceedings 2*, pages 131–146. Springer, 2018.

[58] C. A. Petri. *Kommunikation mit Automaten.* PhD thesis, Universität Bonn, Institut für Instrumentelle Mathematik, Bonn, Germany, 1962.

[59] P. Pilozzi. Automating termination proofs for CHR. In P. M. Hill and D. S. Warren, editors, *ICLP09l*, volume 5649 of *LNCS*, pages 504–508. SV, July 2009.

[60] P. Pilozzi and D. De Schreye. Improved termination analysis of CHR using self-sustainability analysis. In G. Vidal, editor, *LOPSTR11l*, LNCS, 2011.

[61] F. Raiser and T. Frühwirth. Towards term rewriting systems in constraint handling rules. In Schrijvers et al. [65], pages 19–34.

[62] F. Rossi, P. V. Beek, and T. Walsh, editors. *Handbook of Constraint Programming.* Elsevier, 2006.

[63] V. A. Saraswat. *Concurrent Constraint Programming.* MIT Press, 1993.

[64] B. Sarna-Starosta, D. Zook, E. Pasalic, and M. Aref. Relating constraint handling rules to datalog. In Schrijvers et al. [65], pages 127–142.

[65] T. Schrijvers, F. Raiser, and T. Frühwirth, editors. *CHR08l*. RISC Report Series 08-10, University of Linz, Austria, 2008.

[66] J. Sneyers, W. Meert, J. Vennekens, Y. Kameya, and T. Sato. Chr (PRISM)-based probabilistic logic learning. *Theory and Practice of Logic Programming*, 10(4-6):433–447, 2010.

[67] J. Sneyers, T. Schrijvers, and B. Demoen. The computational power and complexity of constraint handling rules. *TOPLAS*, 31(2), February 2009.

[68] J. Sneyers, P. Van Weert, and T. Schrijvers. Aggregates for constraint handling rules. In Duck and Sulzmann [24], pages 91–105.

[69] J. Sneyers, P. Van Weert, T. Schrijvers, and L. De Koninck. As time goes by: Constraint handling rules – a survey of CHR research between 1998 and 2007. *TPLP*, 10(1):1–47, 2010.

[70] I. Stéphan. First-order asp programs as CHR programs. In *Proceedings of the 36th Annual ACM Symposium on Applied Computing*, SAC '21, page 881–888, New York, NY, USA, 2021. Association for Computing Machinery.

[71] L. Sterling and E. Y. Shapiro. *The art of Prolog: advanced programming techniques*. MIT press, 1994.

[72] M. Sulzmann, G. J. Duck, S. Peyton-Jones, and P. J. Stuckey. Understanding functional dependencies via constraint handling rules. *Journal of functional programming*, 17(1):83–129, 2007.

[73] P. Van Weert. Efficient lazy evaluation of rule-based programs. *IEEE Transactions on Knowledge and Data Engineering*, 22(11):1521–1534, November 2010.

[74] P. Van Weert, P. Wuille, T. Schrijvers, and B. Demoen. CHR for imperative host languages. In T. Schrijvers and T. Frühwirth, editors, *Constraint Handling Rules — Current Research Topics*, volume 5388 of *LNAI*, pages 161–212. SV, December 2008.

[75] P. V. Weert, J. Sneyers, T. Schrijvers, and B. Demoen. Extending CHR with Negation as Absence. In *Third Workshop on Constraint Handling Rules*, pages 125–140, Leuven, Belgium, 2006. K.U. Leuven.

[76] J. Widom and S. Ceri. *Active database systems: Triggers and rules for advanced database processing.* Morgan Kaufmann, 1995.

[77] A. Wolf. Adaptive Constraint Handling with CHR in Java. In *Seventh International Conference on Principles and Practice of Constraint Programming*, volume 2239 of *Lecture Notes in Computer Science*, pages 256–270. Springer, 2001.

[78] A. Wolf. Intelligent search strategies based on adaptive constraint handling rules. *Theory and Practice of Logic Programming*, 5(4-5):567–594, 2005.

[79] P. Wuille, T. Schrijvers, and B. Demoen. CCHR: the fastest CHR implementation, in c. In Duck and Sulzmann [24], pages 123–137.

Index